All Happy Families

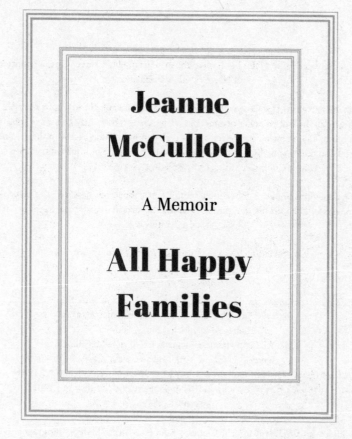

Jeanne McCulloch

A Memoir

All Happy Families

HARPER WAVE

An Imprint of HarperCollins*Publishers*

FIRST HARPER WAVE PAPERBACK EDITION PUBLISHED 2019.

Designed by Fritz Metsch

The Library of Congress has catalogued the hardcover as follows:
Names: McCulloch, Jeanne, author.
Title: All happy families : a memoir / Jeanne McCulloch.
Description: New York : Harper Wave, 2018.
Identifiers: LCCN 2018004273 (print) | LCCN 2018012284 (ebook) | ISBN 9780062234773 (eBook) | ISBN 9780062234759 (hardback) | ISBN 9780062848888 (audio)
Subjects: LCSH: McCulloch, Jeanne. | Editors—United States—Biography. | Periodical editors—United States—Biography. | BISAC: BIOGRAPHY & AUTOBIOGRAPHY / Personal Memoirs. | FAMILY & RELATIONSHIPS / Marriage.
Classification: LCC PN4874.M364 (ebook) | LCC PN4874.M364 A3 2018 (print) | DDC 070.5/1092 [B] —dc23
LC record available at https://lccn.loc.gov/2018004273

ISBN 978-0-06-223476-6 (pbk.)

19 20 21 22 23   LSC   10 9 8 7 6 5 4 3 2 1

Portions of this work have appeared, in slightly different form, in the following publications: in *O Magazine* (2008) in an essay titled "The Maternal Heart" and in *Allure* magazine (2006) in an essay titled "The Perilous Dune," which was also anthologized in *Money Changes Everything: Twenty-Two Writers Tackle the Last Taboo with Tales of Sudden Windfalls, Staggering Debts, and Other Surprising Turns of Fortune* (2007).

Excerpt from *Behind the Lines: The Oral History of Special Operations in World War II* ("I sent one of our GIs ...") by Russell Miller; Macmillan, 2002.

Excerpt from *Drums in the Balkan Night* ("In June 1930, when John ...") by John I. B. McCulloch; G. P. Putnam's Sons, 1936.

For Charlotte and Sam

and in memory of Pierre

Oh as I was young and easy in the mercy of his means,
Time held me green and dying
Though I sang in my chains like the sea.

—DYLAN THOMAS, "Fern Hill"

All happy families are alike; each unhappy family is
unhappy in its own way.

—LEO TOLSTOY, Anna Karenina

Author's Note

I HAVE TRIED to re-create events, locales, and conversations from my memories of them. In some instances, I have changed the names of individuals to protect the privacy of the people involved.

Part
One

· I ·

AUGUST 1983

A WOMAN WALKS into the sea. It's a mid-August day. Early morning. The sky is clear. A mid-August day on the beach near the end of Long Island and it's the summer of 1983. Seagulls idle on the wet sand, and far out the fishing boats from Montauk patrol, small as dark toys against the horizon. It's a perfect late-summer day.

The woman on the shore is my mother. She wears the iconic headdress of her era, a floral bathing cap with brightly colored petals. She walks cautiously, hands out for balance, because even in a calm surf you can't be too careful walking into the sea. She always taught us that. Respect for the sea. The latex petals of the cap flutter about her head, almost festive as she moves. It's early morning and my mother walks into the sea.

Behind her is our house, a long, gray, sea-weathered clapboard house, stretching along a sand dune like a giant sleeping cat. My father bought this house years before the area became known as the Hamptons—back when it was still considered a

long way from New York City, known mainly for artists and
potato fields and the fishermen who made their living trawling
off Montauk Point. The house had a shabby grandeur to it that
time forgot. No air-conditioning ("The sea is our air condi-
tioner!" my mother would proclaim) and no pool ("The sea is
our pool").

Every August when I was young, it was a giant slumber
party in the house by the sea. My sisters and I would fall asleep
against a tumble of cousins in quilts, listening to the steady re-
frain of waves gliding along the shore—the moonlight outside
our bedroom spackling a silver route to the horizon.

August 13, 1983, was the day of my wedding.

I was twenty-five, a messy splatter of freckles across my
nose the final badge of childhood. Just before sunset that afternoon, I would put on a vintage lace dress that swooped gently
off the shoulder in a style I saw as reminiscent of Sophia Loren
in her glory days and my mother saw as suggestive of the sale
rack at a yard sale.

In the house that morning, they were talking in various
rooms. In the pantry, the boy delivering flowers, sprays of lilies of the valley and a basket of rose petals for the wedding
cake, was being bossed around by Johanna, the Irish cook.
Johanna never got to boss anybody in the household; everyone, the housekeeper, the gardener, everyone disregarded her.
She was a small woman in a hairnet, whose wisps of dry black
hair nevertheless escaped and were often found floating in the
vichyssoise. She stamped her foot, a white orthopedic shoe.
"Get out of my kitchen," she was telling the delivery boy from
the florist's shop. "I'm too busy," she scolded him. "Go."

In the sunroom, my half brothers, three men in their early forties, sons from my father's first marriage, huddled in conversation. They all had beards and ready laughs; they—in addition to my half sister—had come for the wedding with their spouses and their children from the far-flung places where they lived lives of their own. Half siblings, and the term was apt; I half knew them, and I half didn't. Scott raised llamas in New Mexico; in Florida, Keith painted lush floral landscapes, some with naked women; in Colorado, Rod was engaged in investment strategies for a business no one understood. Mary Elizabeth, called MB, was an Arabic scholar in Paris. In my father's sunroom, the morning light angled across the sisal rug, dust motes played in the air, and my three half brothers were talking together, shoulders hunched, coffee mugs in hand.

The gardener, Vincent, in yellow protective earmuffs and a fishing cap, drove his seated mower in even rows up and down the sloping lawn, as he did every morning of summer, this day steering around the large white party tent erected earlier in the week for the reception.

My wedding was scheduled to take place at five in the afternoon. It had been timed and debated for months, the proper moment for a wedding. The ceremony was to be situated by the garden up by the house, with a view giving out to the sea. "Situated"—that was the term used by Ruth Ann Middleton, the professional wedding planner my mother had hired to marshal the wedding to perfection. A white wire gazebo had been placed there, and the florist would wreath the lattice in garlands of pink roses.

Five in the afternoon was the time the light would be the rich gold particular to late summer.

A bagpiper in a kilt had been hired by my mother, so at the ceremony's conclusion, he'd guide the guests from the garden down to the tent—braying the union of husband and wife as the setting sun burnished rose through the trees.

"You know, men in kilts don't wear any underwear," my half brother Keith had told us the day before the wedding, as we drove to visit our father. "Seriously, not a stitch. Just a pink ribbon tied around the big fella."

My siblings and I were in the family station wagon when he told us that, on our way to Southampton Hospital. Our father lay in a coma in the ICU, having had a massive stroke two days before the wedding, leaving our home for what we suspected might be the last time strapped to an ambulance stretcher— the strap a thin, final harness to our life. He had had the stroke following an abrupt withdrawal from alcohol after a lifetime of drinking, having gone cold turkey at my mother's insistence so—in her words—he'd "sober up" for the wedding.

On the way to the hospital, Scott had insisted we stop at the fried-chicken place off Route 27, in case we got hungry, and as we stood watching our father breathe, the bucket of chicken sat unopened at the nurses' station of the ICU, filling the air with its irrelevant fragrance.

We had bowed to my mother's insistence that the wedding should go forward, despite our father's condition. Because, she claimed, it's what Daddy would want. "Besides," she added, "all *my* friends are already en route."

And so a man with no underwear, in a plaid skirt, was going to bray on our front lawn at sunset as my father lay in a coma over in the next town.

. . .

The morning of my wedding, an easy breeze blew down the beach. My teenage nephews sat on their surfboards just beyond the break. All was calm and serene from the lilting vantage point of the sea. Occasionally a swell would captivate them and they angled their boards toward the shore, riding in on elegant curls of foam.

Later that afternoon, my mother would pin the family veil on my head. She'd mutter about how I should have let her get a proper hairdresser to tame my wild beach hair. Then she'd call the hospital and instruct them that no matter what happened that evening to her husband, they were not to call our house. Because, she'd go on to say, we were having a party.

The morning of August 13, 1983, the day settled into a steady rhythm near the tip of Long Island. Taking her swim before breakfast, which, she believed, was de rigueur in summertime, my mother walked into the sea.

· II ·

The Wedding Dress

JUNE 1983

IN EARLY JUNE, two months before the wedding, a diminutive woman named Beatrice came at my mother's request to the house by the sea to "do something" about the dress I was wearing for my wedding. "Primp it up somehow," was how my mother put it. "We need to do something," she'd tell Ruth Ann Middleton, the wedding planner, over the phone, and then lower her voice to a small growl: "Dearie, it's a disaster."

I had chosen what my mother called "frankly not much of a dress" to be married in. The dress was soft and old and fragile. It would cinch at the waist in a wide band of lace Beatrice would make. I had chosen pink grosgrain shoes to match, though I wanted red boots and this was our compromise, my mother's and mine. In her opinion, I had chosen something unsuitable to the occasion. Too sexy, too boho, too, to use her expression, tartish. The dress was not one she would have chosen, one of the confections displayed in clear garment bags in the temperature-controlled bridal salons at Bergdorf's, Bonwit's, and Saks. My hippie dress, as she called it, was not her idea of the statement she wanted to make at her eldest daughter's wedding. To her mind, it went with the choice of groom. Not the statement she wanted to make. But even she had to admit, as I tried on dress after dress while she sat on pastel-colored settees outside fitting rooms, waiting, that the entire exercise was all wrong.

"Look at your little face," she said about one. "You are drowning in that dress."

"I feel like a dessert," I admitted. I'd try on another, the bridal advisers buttoning, hooking, smoothing, and smiling.

"Okay," she finally conceded with a sweep of her hand. "I give up. You get your way."

My mother and I did not always get along. There was a time, back when I was about sixteen and her marriage to my father was still fine, that we did. Late at night, we'd sit in the living room of our apartment in New York City in our nightgowns, feet up on the coffee table, drinking diet ginger ale and smoking cigarettes. I had just taken up smoking then, so on those evenings she'd open a long ebony cigarette box she kept on the coffee table, take out a cigarette, and pass the box to me. Then she'd take one of her cherished ceramic lighter holders, each fashioned to look like a small head of romaine lettuce, a disposable Bic lighter nestled inside, and light us up. I was working for a certain look, a sort of controlled nonchalance that I saw my mother as having perfected. The way she'd inhale deeply, raise her chin, and let the smoke drift out in a long dramatic waft. The way she cocked the cigarette between two fingers, her head leaning on a hand, elbow casually resting on the arm of the couch. She looked both wise and elegant to me, even in her nightgown and slippers. Cigarette smoke had such power, I thought. So I puffed when she puffed, exhaled when she did, and listened to her tell me dark stories from the lives of her friends.

Her topic was inevitably men.

"He left her flat," she'd say about one or the other, or "With that weight gain, come on, she had it coming." Above her head the cigarette smoke curled languorously, but her free hand cut the air as she spoke, her brown eyes flashed.

High above the honks and shrieks of the New York City streets, my father and my younger sisters far away in sleep, this is what she taught me: that after the braces, the music lessons, and the first pair of high heels, the next essential item was a man. "Maaahhhn" was how she said it, drawing the syllable out as if it wasn't a word at all but an incantation.

"The army of women" is how she referred to her friends who were divorced or widowed, who were suddenly alone. "Don't be one of the army of women," she'd say, and though I didn't know what she meant, I pictured them all: gray, elegant, with shiny black pocketbooks and Chanel suits, shuffling together past boutique windows on Madison Avenue. I believed her that it was something bad, something to avoid in this world.

But all that was long ago. Long before I met a boy named Dean and let the wild tide of romance funnel into one steady stream. It shattered her very heart, my mother confided to absolutely everyone, that I had never taken an interest in a boy named Eliot whose mother was a friend of hers.

"His family is in the *Social Register*," she would point out, and sigh. It was a fragile sigh, a sigh of maternal resignation, that I could so easily let Eliot and his ilk slip through the family net.

"I suppose I am to blame," she said. "The mother is always to blame. It's our lot."

The *Social Register*, a black book with orange lettering, came in annual hardcover installments and served as a GPS for my mother through the world of New York society. The yearly editions lined the bookshelves behind the couch in our library, within her easy reach. Often she pulled the most recent volume down and studied it, leafing through as one might through a magazine or a catalogue. It was filled with information she found fascinating and valuable, who had gone to what school, what clubs they belonged to, the names of their children, and the names of their houses.

Many families in the pages of the *Social Register* had houses with names. A house with a name spoke of legacy, of a gabled heritage, the faint hint of noble skeletons in every closet. A family seat. Though we had no such heritage, she intended to build one, and she named our house in East Hampton the very first summer we owned it, named it after the street sign she had the gardener erect in the driveway, Children at Play. That name reflected the mandate she bestowed upon herself in marrying my father, an older man whose first wife had divorced him when his children were very young. The Children at Play house was to be the warm cloak under which she gathered his four elder children, now adults, and restored them to him along with their wives and children, to join us every August by the sea.

. . .

In the mid-'60s, East Hampton was a quiet town. The old post office had been converted to a movie theater where the feature changed weekly, and children old enough to ride bicycles could follow a narrow bike path single file under a canopy of giant elm trees all the way into town to spend their allowance at the five-and-ten, or at Marley's stationery store. The houses with names had a steady soundtrack of sprinklers, and the summer air smelled of fresh-cut grass. The drive from New York City took four hours, the final stretch from Southampton along Route 27 past corn and potato fields that in those days gave a view clear to the horizon. At Children at Play my mother saw lawns, with children to run on them, and she saw herself presiding over the extended "clan," as she called it, a nod to the Scottish roots of our last name. She set about posing us in front of the house each summer in clean pressed clothes, smiling for a hired photographer, our mouths open in a semblance of spontaneous laughter. One year someone drove the family car, a Chrysler Imperial convertible with tail fins and push-button gears, onto the front lawn, and we posed in and around it, my parents in the front seat, my mother holding a parasol and my father gripping the wheel, as though we'd all just merrily driven out from the city and somehow missed the driveway and landed square in the middle of the grass. Behind us stood the gray shingled house. Children at Play. She ordered stationery, thick ivory cards with "Children at Play" embossed across the top in bright green print. The name, in Portuguese, was painted on a mosaic of enamel tile that hung over the entryway to the house, "Quinta de Crianças Brincar." My mother's friend Judy had gone to Portugal and brought it back, and to my mother it christened the house with familial vision.

The *Social Register* registered faded love with no apparent hint of irony. Beside the name of any divorced woman, even those remarried, the name of her first husband sat in parentheses, a coded palimpsest for all to see of her romantic past. Beside my mother's name it said "(Van Devere)," referencing a shadowy first husband in Florida never spoken of.

"Eliot Andrews is in law school, and if the truth be known, he has very good genes," she said. "He looks like a young Greek god." She went on, "Please, for me, just think about it. Look at him in profile, dearie, that profile could be on a Greek coin. Strong chin. Nothing out of place."

Where she saw Adonis, I saw Bacchus, a fraternity boy whose chiseled features would swell to paunch and puffiness over time.

"His genes are really like anyone else's, Ma. Levi's."

"Very funny. You have a lot to learn about the world, little thing. A lot to learn about men. Your mother," she'd go on to add, because when she had something important to say, she always referred to herself in the third person, "your mother knows a few things."

"He was a very nice boy for a college romance," was how my mother explained Dean. "You know, the kind of romance a girl should age out of, not marry."

My mother was telling this to Ruth Ann Middleton, her wedding planner. She spoke to Ruth Ann in a British accent. Though she was from Miami, my mother had various accents, and it was the British accent she deployed to speak to Ruth Ann as well as to the ladies from the bridal salons at Saks and Bonwit's and Bergdorf's. In Ruth Ann's case, she added a certain *entre nous* air that sounded less imperious and more clubby, as if, being two women who had memorized entire swaths of the *Social Register*, they could speak to each other from within a sort of gilded cage in confidential tones. Ruth Ann was a large woman with black stubble on her chin. A pocketbook dangled from her forearm at all times, from which she pulled lists and lists of crucial wedding information—caterers, club membership directories, and her contacts at the society desks of key newspapers around the world. Ruth Ann had a credo that weddings start on time. If she was "doing" a wedding, it started when it was supposed to or her name wasn't Ruth Ann Middleton. On her hands, she wore short kid gloves.

"Don't you think the gloves are a bit much?" I'd asked my mother after our first meeting with Ruth Ann.

"Peh," she said. "That girl is a type."

My mother always called women girls, no matter how old.

"What type?"

"They never marry. They compensate by doing other people's weddings. Occupational hazard, I guess. Destined to be one in the army of women."

"A lieutenant in the army of women," I added. "Poor Ruth Ann. Ruth Ann Middleton, lieutenant first class."

"It's sad, dearie," she'd say. "Don't make fun."

It was late June, still a slight chill in the air the morning Beatrice came to "do something" about my dress. A few people walked the beach in sweaters, long pants rolled up their calves, some with dogs trotting alongside.

When she arrived, Beatrice thumped a bolt of lace up the staircase and down the long carpeted hallway to my mother's bedroom. The bedroom was large, with French doors that gave out to a deck with a view to the sea. As the day warmed, a soft wind blew through the open French doors.

Beatrice brought her bolt of lace into the middle of the room and stood beside it, holding it firm so as not to let it teeter and fall. Then she laid the bolt on the rug and unraveled a simple inch, then a yard; finally an intricate pattern emerged, the delicate fabric lopping across the pale pink carpet.

Mostly, looking at the lace that was to cinch my wedding dress, I thought of old aunts with secrets, and spiderwebs, and the passing of time. It smelled softly of tea and roses. I tried to feel respectful of all these meanings, and believe I could wear this delicate lace and pull it off. I had heard tales of girls, girls more sedate than I, losing arms off antique wedding dresses when they started to drink and dance. I was relieved to know there were girls who had dresses that fell apart at their wedding receptions, and yet in their gay dishevelment they went right on.

"This is so feminine," Beatrice said as she looked at the lace, now unfurled along my mother's carpet. To my mother she added, "There is something so feminine about your daughter's taste." She gently shook her head, a quiet gesture of appreciation.

On her head Beatrice wore a purple straw fedora that matched her purple-and-yellow sundress. She wore bright fuchsia lipstick and seemed impatient with my muted tones. "Let's try more color," she suggested quietly, unraveling pink and orange satin sashes she kept neatly coiled at the bottom of her canvas tote.

"All she ever wears is black," my mother agreed. She sat on her bed pulling on the tassel of one of her silk throw pillows. It was an embroidered scene, a prince and princess wearing sil-ver crowns, dismounting from a carriage. Each of her pillows, which ran along the headboard of her bed, depicted a different fairy tale. In another the prince was kissing a sleeping princess while in the background a naked cherub played a lute.

My mother was tall, taller than I; her face had not softened with age but grown more angular, more defined. Her skin was del-icate, aged over time like a sheet washed and dried too many times in the sun. Though now slightly stooped, she still strode with the assurance of someone who held herself strong against the world, someone who was used to getting her own way.

At Children at Play, her bedroom was her command cen-tral. The bed in the room was enormous, two queen beds pushed together, though for years no one had slept in it but her. By her side of the bed, a pink princess phone hung on the wall within easy reach for late-night chats with her sister in Florida or one of her children. Next door, my father slept in his study, adjacent to the bedroom. It was decorated by my mother in a forest green plaid, the shelves and tables filled with his well-thumbed language books, the leather bindings cracked at the spines. My father would spend entire mornings with his books, a can of Budweiser by his side, his glasses in a slow slide down his nose.

My mother's closets were organized by category. One had only tennis dresses, another her entire collection of bright Lilly Pulitzer shifts. Long A-line muumuus that she wore for din-ners at home were hung in a closet with slatted sliding doors for proper ventilation. Another closet was only shoes, mounted vertically on shelves so that the shoes—flat sandals in shades to match the Lillys, a few grass-stained Tretorn tennis sneakers, satin slingbacks, and white summer pumps—appeared to be climbing the wall. Another closet was arranged in color-coded stacks of sweaters and sharkskin slacks for colder summer days. The doorknob of the tennis dress closet was employed to hang a necklace made up of numerous strands of tiny freshwater pearls, hung there to keep the strands from getting into the frenzied tangle that would be inevitable if left to their own devices. When she wore it, as she did often in the summer, the eruption of pearls hung in tiers of zany frivolity from her neck and looked, my sisters and I would tell her, as if an oyster had had multiple orgasms on her chest.

"I'm wearing blue to the wedding," my mother told Beatrice as she pulled on the tassel.

Beatrice nodded. "That's a lovely color for the mother of the bride," she purred encouragingly.

"Not really a robin's egg," my mother went on, "but darker, an almost, I don't know, a no-color blue."

"That doesn't make any sense," I said. I was standing at the mirror, a sash of cantaloupe silk looped around my waist over my jeans. I looked to the dressmaker. "Beatrice, does that make any sense to you? 'No-color blue'?"

"Oh," she replied. She spoke softly. "Every color is a color. Blue is one of our very true colors. We depend on blue." She looked at the silk tassel my mother was worrying with her hand. "That, for example, is a periwinkle. From the periwinkle family. A periwinkle is also a very true blue."

My mother did not like to be corrected, particularly by someone she was paying to be agreeable. "No-color blue," she repeated. "It's the color of my dress for the wedding." She flitted her hand. "A color worn only by me." She looked at the clock at her bedside.

"Let's get this done with," she said, "Betty."

Though the dressmaker's name was not Betty but Beatrice, my mother had persisted in calling her Betty since the day I found my wedding dress at her shop in SoHo in the late spring.

"Peh, come on," she had said to me that day as I rode uptown with her in a cab. "She's an out-and-out Betty, there's nothing even remotely Beatrice about that girl. She's just trying to be pretentious." She looked down at her manicure as she spoke. "She's a very common girl, if the truth be known."

We drove another ten blocks or so, the cab threading through the late-morning traffic. "And, I might add, I am not an 'automatic Pat.'"

"A who?"

"You heard her, don't act like you didn't. As soon as she saw my name on the checkbook, she took it upon herself to call me Pat."

I had heard her, and my heart had frozen when Beatrice called her Pat. There were certain things guaranteed to irk my mother, things other people would never imagine gave offense, like taking a seat on what she considered her side of our living room couch, or saying "folks" when you meant "people" or "drapes" when you meant "curtains" or "hose" when you meant "stockings" or "gift" when you meant "present." The "automatic Pat" offense was the worst of them. Beatrice now was sunk, and try as I might, I would never be able to redeem her in my mother's opinion.

"Ma, to be fair, it is your name."

"Not automatically it's not. I'm Mrs. McCulloch until such

time as I say otherwise. As, I can assure you, I will not in the case of this girl Betty who owns a thrift store in the bowels of SoHo."

She watched out the window, hands in her lap, one gesturing ever so slightly from time to time. It was a vague twitch her thumb and forefinger made, rising up in sudden small darts from her lap. This was evidence that she was carrying on a conversation in her head, often in French. Clearly she had a few more words for an imaginary Beatrice that required a change to a more imperious language. My mother's spoken French was not entirely fluent, but when she constructed imaginary conversations in French in her head, her command of the language was perfect and her repertoire full of chilling *mots justes*.

After a time, she took my hand. "Listen to me," she said. "Listen to your old ma. We're going to get through this damn thing with grace and style, baby girl, even if it kills us."

Apparently I owe my entire existence to a ladies' lunch that took place late in 1956. My mother was reluctant to have children. So the story went, at least. She was thirty-seven when she had me, a relatively unusual age to be having a first child in the late 1950s. According to legend (a.k.a. my mother's college friend Nancy), my entire conception, not the act, of course, but the promulgation of the act, was decided over lunch on the Upper East Side of Manhattan sometime late in 1956. My father had proposed to her the day earlier, in a taxicab going over the Triborough Bridge, and in a panic my mother convened her two best friends, Nancy and Mu. I don't know what they ate, but I do know they were at Gino's, which was in its day an institution: a classic Italian spot on the Upper East Side that drew a regular crowd from its opening in 1945 until its ultimate closing in 2010. The décor never changed; zebras (allegedly 108 of them) leapt along on a tomato-red background on the signature wallpaper that ran from the kitchen in the back all the way to the front door. The menu never changed from classic Italian red-sauce fare, and the clientele ranged from a handful of local celebrities to tourists hoping to spot them, and a steady inflow of the East Side ladies who lunched (it was after all just up the block from Bloomingdale's). Hence the three-way huddle in 1956.

At thirty-seven my mother had black hair that she wore in bangs across her forehead and in an even row of flip curls along her jawline. She was working in the publicity department at Dior, and shared an apartment with Mu in the East 50s. They were two bachelorettes in careers in Midtown at a time where women in their late thirties were usually long settled. The fact that she was probably, if you do the math, which I did as soon as I knew how many months it took to have a baby, already pregnant with me notwithstanding, she was apparently in need of counsel. Marrying an older man who did not work concerned her, is how the story went, and her two lifelong friends, Nancy and Mu, talked her into it.

A word about these women at this ladies' lunch. They had met at Sweet Briar College in the '40s and liked to refer to themselves, with a nod to Gilbert and Sullivan, as "the three little maids from school." Nancy, who was short and sassy, was a journalist at *Life* magazine. She was married to a famous journalist of the day, though he would be only the first of five husbands. Mu—her real name was Muriel, but she couldn't stand it and preferred this moniker suggestive of a cow—had long, luxurious brown hair she wrapped in a twist on her head. At the time of the ladies' lunch, Mu had met and later married a lawyer she originally came to know because my mother had so many parking tickets, she had hired him to get her off the hook. When he did, she brought him back to the apartment she and Mu shared for a celebratory drink. He took one look at Mu, with her mane of hair and hourglass curves, and fell instantly in love. Nancy and Mu regularly came with their husbands to visit us at the house by the sea, and the three women would do exercise classes together on the lawn, poking their pedicured pink toes into the air for a few minutes to tone their legs, then breaking for a cigarette. Nancy wore a bikini and her reading glasses all day long until it was time to dress for dinner, when they all three put on brightly colored muumuus. In the evenings, they played hands of bridge with the husbands, or bent over one of the thousand-piece jigsaw puzzles on a yellow table by the piano.

Back in 1956, at a November conference at Gino's, the advice from Nancy and Mu would translate in today's argot roughly as "Go for it, girl. Have the baby, marry the man, have more babies—it's now or never, if you catch our drift."

So I was born, and my two sisters followed in relatively quick succession. As creation myths go, we all three owe our lives to a ladies' lunch in 1956 at Gino's.

· III ·

CAMDEN, MAINE, AUGUST 11, 1983

IN CAMDEN, MAINE, two days before the wedding, my future mother-in-law, Helen Jackson, sat on her bed in the early morning, surrounded by piles of clothes. Her dress for the wedding was laid out on the bed. It was silk, and it was one she hoped would coordinate with the dress my mother was wearing. All my mother had said about her own dress was "no-color blue." Whatever that meant. Helen thought this might be a dodge to confuse her. "No color" was not a color. She was a home economics major from Skidmore, class of 1953, and there was not a color called "no color." She would bet her diploma on it.

They would never be friends, these mothers, but Helen was determined to be cooperative. The dress she had chosen was the color of a tropical sea, and from her background, she knew the color of her own dress had a name. Sea foam. It had a high collar and a scarf that looped around the neck and tied in a loose cravat under her chin. The dress offset her light gray hair. "I think I could have fun in it," she'd told me over the phone. She'd laughed and raised her voice to a lilt: "Comfort and ease, that's all I asked for in a dress, honey. That's how to have real fun."

Camden, a harbor town on the Maine coast eighty-five miles north of Portland, was where my fiancé, Dean, grew up. The main street through town hugged the harbor, with small shops on either side punctuated by Cappy's Chowder House just off the town landing. The view from the window booth at Cappy's looked out on the town dock, where at day's end lobstermen in rubber overalls docked to unload their bounty from traps all over Penobscot Bay. Black lobsters squirmed in bundles of fishing net on the dock at sundown.

Dean's family lived in a white saltbox house just a quarter mile up Route 1 from the center of town. On the third floor, up a narrow flight of stairs, the view from a tiny triangular window in the attic gave out onto Camden Harbor. On a clear day, the boats anchored to the town slips were visible, their masts switching rhythmically in the current.

Helen's husband, Raymond, my future father-in-law, had packed for the wedding easily, promptly. He was like that; he packed very little, and he packed efficiently, folding everything into the smallest possible duffle. A Navy man, Raymond had spent his early adult life on the sea, and from that experience he had developed an appreciation for efficiency, for punctuality, and a fondness for PET milk.

Raymond and Helen were leading a caravan of cars, neighbors they'd invited to the wedding from Camden, down Route 1 to I-95 to New London. Helen and Raymond and their "hard core," as they called them, their closest friends in Camden, Don and Nelly, Rick and Jan. There they'd meet up at the ferry dock with Helen's brother, Phil, and his wife, Anita, who were bringing Helen's mother, called Nonnie, from Westerly, Rhode Island. They'd ride across the Long Island Sound together, the "hard core" drinking beers and eating hot dogs on the deck while the cars sloshed in the hold below. The directions to the house sounded simple enough: follow Route 114 all the way from the dock in Orient Point across Shelter Island and into East Hampton, take a right as the road ends, continue around the slight bend on Ocean Avenue, turn right onto Lily Pond Lane. Raymond had it all clear in his mind and timed, but they could not miss their ferry or there would be hell to pay. They'd not easily get four cars onto another one in the middle of August, the height of tourist season, and who could say they wouldn't have to pay extra for rescheduled reservations.

As long as things stayed on schedule, Raymond believed, life proceeded as planned with no curveballs. Raymond was not big on curveballs.

Sitting on her bed, trying to pack for the wedding, Helen warded off panic. She called me on the phone.

"I want to be on board for all this, honey," she told me. "Meanwhile Raymond Jackson is downstairs having a fit that I'm not ready."

I pictured her, phone wire dangling, seated on the patchwork bedspread of their four-poster bed with her clothes all around her, Raymond pacing in the front hall below.

"'No color,'" she said, lowering her voice a register, as if with each breath losing confidence. "I mean, let's just start right there. Oh, brother."

"Mother!" Raymond called up the stairs. Ever since they'd first had children, Raymond called his wife Mother and not by her name. She in turn often called him Daddy. "Mother!" Raymond called. "There's a ferry to catch. Damn it."

"O-kay," she shouted, and then to me she sighed, "Let the show begin."

The first time I visited Camden, I got a new name. "This is the city girl," Helen would say, introducing me around to the butcher, the greengrocer, the postal clerk, her hand resting lightly on my back.

"Can I ask a city girl to pick beans?" I overheard her say one day on the phone. She was at the kitchen table with her back to me as she said this, sliced apples for pie in a bowl at her side. The afternoon sun was in a golden slant across the linoleum floor, and the room smelled clean and fresh from the fruit.

As I walked in, she turned and waved, but there was never any more talk about the beans. Apparently, she decided way back then I was not the bean-picking type.

"'City girl,' please," my mother commented after my first visit to Camden. She called in from Paris, where my parents had rented a flat on the Place du Marché Saint-Honoré, a small cul-de-sac where the smell of fresh bread floated up from the boulangerie down the block in the mornings, and where, because it was a weekend, I could hear the distant cries of the *footballeurs* in the background practicing on the roof of the parking garage across the street. "*Merde*," they were crying, and "*Pas ma faute!*"

"Did you tell her about all your summers? What about when you girls were with Marie-Jeanne in the Valais?"

One summer when we were teenagers, my sisters and I were sent to stay with the family of our au pair, Marie-Jeanne, who lived in the Valais, a narrow valley in the French part of Switzerland, streaked with knotty grapevines and hillsides dotted with milk cows. Although in truth we only visited for a week, my mother often credited that journey as proof of our credentials as French-speaking country girls. Marie-Jeanne had a brother, François, who had given me my first taste of wine and later my first kiss.

In June, in the Valais, women and children go to pick strawberries from the patches around the canton. Strong, ruddy women hike up their skirts, crouch low to the ground, and gather the berries into rumpled paper bags brought from home. Children race between the rows of bushes, staining clothes and knees a muddy red.

"They act like you had a subnormal childhood. Which you did not. Not if I had anything to do with it. Worrying about the picking of beans. You've picked berries in languages they've never even heard of, baby girl. Beans. Have you ever."

All in all, I'd had seven visits to Camden by the time of Dean's and my wedding. After the visit of the beans, there was the visit of the dead cat, when the wife of the high school basketball coach got Mook, the family tabby, mixed up in the dryer with the wet sheets. Then there was the visit on the lake, when one summer Raymond and Helen rented a cabin on Lake Megunticook and it rained all week and everyone got sick. After that, there was the visit of the divorces, when the minister of the Congregational church in town, the "Congo," came out of the closet and moved in with a young man from Belfast, and Raymond and Helen's friends Rick and Jan broke up for a few chaotic months after a weekend at an EST retreat, leaving kids confused and scattered all over Helen's living room. Through it all Helen made fudge and cheese sticks, and the fifth visit was the visit of the games: Trivial Pursuit, Fictionary, charades, every night after dinner. "Oh, I love it," Helen would cry, her hand coming down hard on her thigh, full of the spirit of combat and red wine. "I love a good game." The sixth visit was the visit of the camping trip, when Dean and I spent two days at Baxter State Park. We hiked long trails Dean knew by heart from his boyhood. I followed behind, and in his casual assurance as he walked the familiar area I found a kind of peace. We slept curled in an embrace in a tent by a pond, and in the clear morning air made pancakes from a mix over a campfire, scrutinized by a family of deer.

Often when we visited, Raymond and Helen drove down Route 1 to Portland to pick us up at the bus station. They tended to do something cute together on the way down. One year they did all their Christmas shopping at L.L.Bean. Another year they walked the beach in Small Point with a bottle of bourbon and a transistor radio.

My seventh visit was the visit of the moonstones, when Dean and I sailed over to nearby Barred Island and anchored for a night in the cove. On the coarse brown sand, there were moonstones. The stones were smooth and jet-black, gleaming when wet like the backs of the harbor seals. The flat, wide ones made the best skippers, Dean told me. He showed me how to hold the stone in the crook of my hand between thumb and forefinger, cock my wrist back, and snap it so the stone launched level over the surface of the water. Upon contact, the moonstone skimmed the glassy surface in quick hops, first making big splashes, then smaller and smaller, finally infinitesimal ones before slipping underwater into the bay.

When he was younger, Dean and his father used to sail over to Barred Island and stand at the shore skipping stones together, the two of them side by side discussing school life (Dean) and town news (Raymond), eyes steady on the water and arms swinging.

"The record's sixteen," he told me.

"Sixteen skips, with one rock?"

"Stone."

"Stone."

As he demonstrated the technique, skipping stones over and over, I stood beside him and drew Christmas trees in the wet sand with my toe. He could throw stones in the water forever, I began to think. I put a handful of moonstones in my pocket and we walked along the beach, the stones lightly knocking against my thigh as we walked. That night we slept on the boat, anchored in the quiet. The moon was a crescent, and there were hundreds of stars out, turning the sky milky.

One day, Raymond had told us, he wanted grandchildren so he could teach them how to navigate by the stars. "Boat-nut grandkids" is what he called them. I pictured them all, with broad, featureless faces like moons. They'd be seated with Raymond in a rowboat, and they'd follow his arm up as he pointed to the sky. "This is how we do it," he'd be telling them. "This is how we learn to be guided by stars."

Dean and I lay on our backs on the deck of the boat in the cove that night, a lantern hung on the mast for light. For a while when he was nineteen Dean worked on a boat. There were ten of them on that boat then, ten young men growing their first beards, carrying cargo back and forth between ports of call in the Caribbean. Talking about it, Dean got a relaxed, dreamy look on his face, remembering the warm tropical sun, the constant slap and splash of the current against the boat, the easy, jostling friendships he developed then. When we were out on a night filled with stars, he would talk about the hours he spent on watch: just him, the deck, the water, the sky, when everything in his life was just about to happen.

Sometimes, when he looked up at the stars, I knew Dean was back on his cargo boat. He'd smile, but it would always end with a long sigh. What is nostalgia, anyway. It isn't happy; it's a tug at the heart. "I was so young then," he'd say, even though it was only six years ago. Now, as he watched, he could see the long, mysterious edges of his life neatly folding in.

After Dean fell asleep, I took one of the moonstones I'd been keeping in my pocket and launched it out into the quiet of the night. It didn't skip, exactly, but made a huge splash upon hitting the water, hopped once, and promptly sunk. Hearing the splash, Dean jolted suddenly, thinking something had gone overboard, something was awry. It was the quick reflex of a sailor, trained to keep a weather eye even in sleep. But of course everything was fine, still intact, same as usual, and soon he settled back into dreams. Only the dark water still recorded the splashes. Where everything in the cove at Barred Island had once been peaceful, serene, suddenly the reflections of lantern, the moon, the night sky all trembled, in the water, with worry.

In marrying Dean, I had chosen to marry the boy next door, in the sense that he lived in the room next door to mine in college.

It was not the next door my mother had had in mind all the years she spent daydreaming with the *Social Register* in her lap, but it was the next door I chose.

Dean was a tall boy with dark curls I had first seen loping across our college campus with engineering books and a silver earring in his left lobe. We had never much spoken until a week before graduation, when we stayed up all one night explaining our senior theses to each other. I tried to explain all British and American literature since 1910, making a chaos of books I pulled from my shelves and laid open on the bed, and he explained Einstein's theory of relativity. I read him small offerings of T. S. Eliot and Virginia Woolf as he lay propped on my pillows listening, his long legs crossed at the ankles, wearing nubby rag socks too warm for the early June evening. By the time the birds were announcing the coming day, we'd moved the discussion into my bed. I liked his cleft chin and his whisper in the dark. Even if what he was whispering that first night was *E equals m c-squared*. And I liked that he played the entire Joni Mitchell songbook on his guitar in the campus coffeehouse wearing a bandanna on his head. This tall boy with a soft whisper in the dark and an earring in his left lobe, this Maine boy destined for a lab coat had my heart.

Somewhere along the line, between the visit of the lake and the visit of the divorces, I erected a white picket fence in my mind around Dean and his family, around the whole town of Camden, and I wanted to be on the inside of that fence, where the kitchen always smelled like fresh fruit pies baking and the afternoon sun glazed the old linoleum floor the color of marigolds; where the view from the top of the attic stairs gave out onto the harbor and from there to Penobscot Bay. Dean had been the local high school basketball champion, and people still stopped him on the street in town to recount match highlights from his winning season senior year. His family sang songs at night, Dean and his brothers all tenors, Raymond a bass, his sister a soprano. "Sit next to me," Helen would say, "I'm singing closest to your range," and I'd sit, Helen's rich alto in my ear, and try to follow her lead.

The visit on the lake, Helen knit me a sweater.

"I'm here with my city girl," she said to Marjorie in the wool shop as we walked in, the bell above the door clanging as she flung it open. The sweater was a deep claret red. She knit it during the long rainy week on Lake Megunticook, sitting in an easy chair by the wood-burning stove. "I think you could have fun with this," she said, her mouth a gentle smile. I watched as the rich red yarn took form. Something fun. Something warm.

On the bulletin board above the sewing table off the kitchen, Helen had a pamphlet from Skidmore College featuring a 1950s-era black-and-white photograph of girls in white tunics seated in neat rows of austere wooden desks.

"What is home economics?" the pamphlet asked. And answered, "It is the field of study dealing with the management of the home and its place in the broader community."

Helen's father, Lester Greene, used to joke that Helen's Skidmore piecrust, a family favorite, was the most expensive piecrust recipe in the entire world. "Hope you all like it," he'd tell guests, "because it cost me dearly. Four years' college tuition. That damn piecrust."

Helen and her mother, Nonnie, each had a metal file box with the family recipes written out on index cards. At the bottom of each card, they signed their name. It was their work of art. When Dean and I got engaged, they made me one. It was in gray metal file boxes that family secrets were handed down, one generation to the next, the most coveted being Lester Greene's recipe for a clambake. You had to marry into the family to get that one.

On the index card Helen gave me with her piecrust recipe, she had added a note: "Patch as much as you need; it doesn't hurt." And then she signed it, as she did all her recipe cards, "H. Jackson."

I'd watch her knitting needles fly as my sweater grew in her lap. What could I say, I wondered, what could anyone say, to Helen's carefully patterned, deliberate life. She had drawn her children safe within her white picket fence, where she fed them pie and knit them sweaters. To my mind, the gate around that fence was always welcoming, and always secure. Family secrets involved flour and shortening and the correct layering of seafood in a pot, not assumed foreign accents and cans of Budweiser at breakfast. I wanted in.

Ever since Dean's younger brother, Chris, left for college, Raymond and Helen had lived in the family house alone.

For a while Dean worried about his parents, on their own suddenly in the house after the bustle of family life, and he called all the time to check in. "What are you up to?" he'd ask. "What have you two fuds been doing?"

"Oh, just running around the house naked," Raymond would say, "isn't that right, Mother?" On another extension, Helen would laugh.

The thought of Raymond with his spindly legs, his gold spectacles, his slight paunch, and Helen, large, white, square, running naked through the halls of his childhood home didn't amuse Dean. "Fact is," he'd tell me when he'd hang up, "it's really not as funny as they think."

Helen kept a photograph in a silver frame on her mahogany dresser. It was a black-and-white photo of her and Raymond during their courtship, seated at a white cast-iron table in Nonnie's garden. Helen is in a stiff organdy dress, Raymond in his white Navy uniform. Raymond holds his teacup in his hands and smiles. Some of these details are timeless: the platter of raw vegetables with Nonnie's special curry pineapple dip, the alabaster garden ornaments, cherubs in balletic poses among the hydrangeas. The photograph is taken from above, so Nonnie must have been spying on them, peeking out from her bedroom window to snap the photograph because it was such an occasion. Young Raymond Jackson, a Harvard man, was back in town from the Naval Academy in Annapolis, and he was there in her garden with her only daughter, having afternoon tea. And her heart always fluttered, Nonnie's did, when she saw a man in a uniform.

The night before our wedding, the rehearsal dinner, was to be Raymond and Helen's evening. They had planned a traditional New England clambake on the beach in front of the long gray house by the sea. Helen had spoken at length to John Haessler, the owner of the Seafood Shop, whose staff would be replicating what, in the Jackson family, was known only as "Grampa's Bake." Offered up to their new family, Dean's future in-laws, the bake was, in Jackson family terms, an offering of their heart.

In Dean's family, there was a strict order to this bake. Key placement was the lobster. Years of experience had taught Helen's father, Lester Greene, the founder of the family recipe, that the lobster gets overcooked if it's put at the bottom.

"Most people make this common mistake," Helen told Haessler. "It's important you place the lobsters on top." She asked him to take notes as she went on. "Then, when unpacking the bake, put the lobsters between layers of hot rockweed to keep them warm for serving last. That last note is very important to get right."

Raymond and Helen had mailed the family recipe to Haessler, and it arrived at his shop on Route 27 with a note stapled on top saying, "If you guys follow this, you cannot go wrong. Trust us Mainiacs!" and Raymond and Helen both signed their names.

"We serve up a lot of meals this way, ma'am," Haessler had assured Helen on the phone after reviewing her instructions. John and his partner, Robert Wilford, were two local schoolteachers who had started their business in a little shop on the main route east between Wainscott and East Hampton in 1972. Until then the only places that serviced the towns were miles and miles away, in Montauk and in Three Mile Harbor.

"A bake is not just a meal, though, my good man," Helen emphasized to the caterer. "It's a gala event. We're talking here about giving up an entire day. In our family, we find it's best to plan and sleep by the site."

It was one of the things Helen missed most, clambakes on the beach when her children were young, when they'd bring enough blankets and sleeping bags to camp by the fire and watch the stars. She and Raymond would sit together by the fire, the kids curled up nearby in their sleeping bags. They would lean in against each other, one blanket draped over both their shoulders, and watch the sleeping bodies of their children rise and fall with each breath as slowly the embers died.

On the roof of the family station wagon, Raymond had tied a brand-new green canoe. Raymond was a snob about boats. He readily admitted that. After the Navy, he had started a publishing career based on wooden boats—writing magazine articles about them, publishing books about them, as well as sailing in them—and to his mind the only acceptable water-going vessel was made of wood. That said, the canoe on the top of the car was fiberglass so it would be lightweight enough to be portable. Around its midsection at Helen's insistence he had tied streamers of green and yellow ribbon, thick ribbons three inches wide so the effect would make a festive statement as they arrived in East Hampton, rounding the long driveway that curved up to the house with a boat on the roof, ribbons flapping.

In the back of the station wagon, Helen had placed a picnic basket with matching ribbons tied in a bow and two life preservers in clear plastic wrappers. She'd bought a card with a watercolor image of the Owl and the Pussy-cat from the bookshop in town. "Kids," Helen wrote on the card, "To get you started on your journey together, a beautiful pea green boat."

She folded her belongings into her suitcase. Bathing suit, tennis whites, slacks and a sweater, because at night it would be cold. She had knit a wool shawl to wear the night of the wedding, creamy white angora wool, using a dainty loose stitch, with a delicate gold filigree piping along the edge. It was to go over her sea-foam dress. It would be a fun look.

. . .

Setting out for the wedding, a green canoe decorated in long ribbons strapped on the roof of their car, Raymond wanted no curveballs, and Helen wanted to have fun. Later they would look back at the photographs from the wedding and Helen would say, "Daddy looks old and I look fat." Her mother, Nonnie, would frame only the photograph of the table setting, a picture of a round table set for ten, pearl-white plates with gold trim on a white damask tablecloth, pink napkins; clear green bud vases held baby-pink roses and sprays of lilies of the valley and were placed beside each napkin. She had sent her youngest grandson, Chris, down to take the photograph of the tables while everyone else was still up in the garden. She wanted to be sure he snapped it, she said, before the festivities began and the tables got all mussed by guests eating and drinking and kicking up their heels. She wanted to have a picture of the perfect table setting to remember Dean's wedding by.

On the mantel in her living room, Nonnie lined up photographs of table settings from each of the family weddings. She knew which table setting belonged to which wedding. So if a visitor pointed, she could say whose wedding it had been. It was important to remember that because, she said, a marriage may not last forever, and then no matter how beautiful it was, what do you do with the picture? Who needs a photograph of someone's ex on the mantel? A table setting, though. That's something else. A table setting is forever.

TO: *John Haessler, The Seafood Shop, Wainscott, NY*
FROM: *Raymond and Helen Jackson, 34 High Street,*
    Camden, Maine 04843
RE: *McCulloch beachfront clambake 8/12/83*

Jackson Family Bake

Serves 18 (adjust amounts as necessary pending final head count)

16 quarts soft-shell steam clams
water to cover
3 tablespoons vinegar
18 potatoes in their jackets
18 ears of sweet corn on the cob
18 flounder filets
36 link sausages
melted butter
18 lobsters
1 bushel rockweed from clean salt water
1 large potato
1 quart water

About 4 hours before baking time, cover the clams with water, and the vinegar, and stir well. This makes the clams throw off sand and does not alter the taste. Scrub the potatoes, leaving the skins on. Husk and desilk the corn, removing all but the innermost layer. Roll each filet around 2 sausages, then wrap the filets in Patapar paper. Divide the steamers in thirds and put each portion in a gauze bag for ease in removing from the bake.

For the cooking, use a large, heavy-duty metal refuse can, with its cover, over an open grate or an improvised fireplace made of cinder blocks. Devise a rack about 4 inches high that will raise the bake above the juices. Pack in this order (which makes it come in almost the right order for serving, see note): layer of rockweed, fish-and-sausage packages, rockweed, sweet corn, rockweed, potatoes, layer of rockweed, bags of clams, rockweed, live lobsters, rockweed. This fills the can. In the top layer of rockweed, bury the large potato as a timer. Put the quart of water in the can, cover it, and set it over the fireplace. Make a brisk fire underneath, and keep the fire going until the bake is done. Note when steam begins to come out around the cover. Approximately one hour and ten minutes from this time the bake should be done. If the potato on the top is not well-done, cook a while longer until it is. Remove the can from the fire.

Each course should be served hot to be best.

First course: clams with melted butter
Second course: potatoes, sweet corn, and the fish-and-sausage rolls
Third course: lobsters with melted butter. Each lobster should be split open and the claws given a breaking crack to make it easier to get the meat out.
Dessert course: fruit pies, use following recipe for crusts

NOTE: Experience has taught that the lobster gets overcooked if put at the bottom of the bake. Put the lobster on top. When unpacking the bake, put the lobsters between two layers of hot rockweed to keep them warm for serving last.

Skidmore College Piecrust

(adjust amounts per number of pies)

2 cups flour
1 teaspoon salt
2/3 cup Crisco
1/3 cup cold water

Mix the flour and salt in a large mixing bowl. Cut in 1/3 cup Crisco well until it looks like coarse meal. Cut in another 1/3 cup Crisco until the mixture forms large chunks. With a fork, mix in 1/3 cup cold water.

Roll this. It makes a double large pie.

NOTE: patch as much as you need; it doesn't hurt.

· IV ·

The Spy Who Loved Me

MY FATHER HAD a favorite story he used to tell. He told it for guests, rising to his feet at the head of the family dinner table, his wineglass up in a toast. The story is about two mice who one day find themselves cornered by a vicious cat. As the first mouse cowers, certain the jig is up, the second mouse looks the cat straight in the eye and bellows: *"Bow wow wow!"* The cat, terrified, runs away. Astonished, the first mouse asks the second, "My good fellow, how ever did you manage that?" to which the second replies: "Simple. It always pays to have a second language."

Hyperpolyglot: one who speaks many languages.

My father collected words. He spoke as many as fourteen languages, and when he wasn't at home studying them, he was traveling abroad to use them in their native context. Many he had fluently, including French, Italian, Spanish, German, Hungarian, Russian, Serbo-Croatian, Swedish, and Polish. Others he categorized as "I can get by in conversation and if need be argue my point." Some were relegated to "taxi and restaurant" languages, meaning he only had enough to get where he needed to go and order food. Some he had "book fluency" in—he could not converse but could translate from that language to English on paper. Some he didn't speak at all but knew how to write, such as classical Arabic and Mandarin.

My father had grown up in the Midwest of the early twentieth century. He was a quiet, patient boy from St. Louis, Missouri, whose grandfather John I. Beggs had been a business associate of Thomas Edison, and thus in the right place at the right time to become a multimillionaire utilities magnate in the early twentieth century. His daughter, my grandmother Mary Grace Beggs, married Richard McCulloch of United Railways, a pioneer of electric train transportation. Thus, electricity and railroads formed a major merger, and my father was the offspring. This was all lore by the time it was handed down to us, but for my father and his two siblings, it meant that the life they led was formal and free of financial worry. One dressed for dinner, children were to be seen and not heard, parents were called Mother and Father and one appeared before them at the proper instances, all this regulated by a team of governesses who did the actual nuts-and-bolts parenting—tending to baths and skinned knees and meals and toothaches and bad dreams. To one's parents one spoke formally and only when spoken to. Summers were spent on a lake in Wisconsin called Oconomowoc, where the family owned their own island, known as Beggs Isle, and all supplies were brought by boat to a grand house where three generations of the Beggs family resided. In photos, my father and his sister and brother are dressed in starched outfits, my aunt Sally with a big bow in her hair, my father and my uncle Robert in ties and short pants. They pose with vacant stares under a vast weeping willow.

Many times, I've wished I could locate that young child and see, as he grew, how the quest to master new languages fired his imagination and grew along with him. How he developed his gift of communication when he was not allowed to speak unless spoken to. He was by all accounts a shy boy, growing up in impersonal and joyless luxury, and I wonder where the love of foreign languages took root. Was the gift of communication a dodge, a way to deflect his own feeling? Was it easier to speak in foreign languages than to speak from the heart? Or a code he adopted to speak truth to power—power being the distant and affectless adults—in ways they could not understand? Was communication in foreign languages to foreigners a way to reach out past his upbringing, to learn to express in code that which he did not feel license to express in his native tongue?

These secrets of the past that can only be pieced together through a few stories handed down through the generations, through boxes of photographs, books left on shelves, a suitcase of old letters.

My father entered Yale at sixteen and tucked a number of graduate degrees under his belt by the time, in his late twenties, he departed with his young first wife on a three-year honeymoon exploring the Balkans. It was 1936, and the region, only recently opened at that time to the West, became the subject of the only book he ever wrote, *Drums in the Balkan Night*.

The author's bio on the back reads:

In June 1930, when John I. B. McCulloch was graduated from Yale, he left the same night for a trip around the world. The following winter he spent in India where he studied Hindustani in Delhi, met Gandhi in Allahabad and Rabindranath Tagore at his school north of Calcutta. The next spring found him in China. The school year of 1931–32 he studied at New College, Oxford, and learned Arabic and Persian, among other things. For two months in the autumn of 1932 he was in Moscow and saw the celebration for the 15th anniversary of the October Revolution. In 1932–33 he was in Paris studying at the École Libre des Sciences Politiques. In September 1934, he married Elizabeth Ten Broeck Jones of Milwaukee and since then, most of their time has been spent in Eastern Europe.

In the photo on the frontispiece, he is in shirtsleeves, his hair blowing in the wind, his young wife, Betty, in white shorts, a halter top, and white pumps. He would have been twenty-eight. He is lanky, his face thin, a radiant smile exposing a row of straight white teeth. They appear to be on the deck of a cruising vessel; behind them is a rail, and beyond that the Aegean Sea. He quotes a line of Aubrey Herbert in his book, a line that, he writes, always thrilled him: "I went to the East by accident, as a young man might go to a party, and find his fate there."

I've thought of that line often over the years. The whimsicality, the spirit of adventure, the openness to fate wherever it might lead. "As a young man might go to a party"—the party being in my father's case the world unfolding in the wake of World War II, where fate defined an entire generation.

After their return from the Balkans, Betty gave birth to their four children in quick succession and America joined the war. Recruited to the Office of Strategic Services, or OSS, my father served as an intelligence officer during the war, and in the immediate aftermath as a kind of multilingual peace-keeping force of one.

He always spoke modestly of "summoning up" a language, as if he had but to call on one and it appeared on the tip of his tongue. Language primers, the language of each written on the spine, lined the rows of our family bookshelves, and I pictured this shelf whenever he spoke of summoning a language to the fore—Arabic, Hebrew, Modern Persian, Old English, Finnish, Welsh, Icelandic, Urdu, Romanian, Chinese. *Jifunze Kiingereza* was a primer on teaching English to native Swahili speakers. Yoruba was the mother tongue of certain regions of Western Nigeria.

"Summoning up my best Yoruba" would not be an unusual thing to hear my father say at the start of a story.

Even when at times they didn't share anything else—dreams, secrets, opinions, or a bed—my parents shared the couch in the library of our apartment. On the bookshelf that spanned the wall behind the couch, my father's language books lined the rows on his side much as the *Social Register* lined the rows on hers. These volumes lived side by side for as long as my parents did—the regimented black spines of New York social hierarchy and his textbooks, all different sizes, some leather-bound and some paperbacks, some tall, some short and thick, quite a few first edition hardbacks, their covers chipped from use.

The details of my father's life in the OSS came out only in small increments. Some nights when they had dinner guests he'd rise to his feet and sing the German ballad "Lili Marlene" in the original German, explaining he'd learned it from a double agent in Berlin at the end of the war—a female double agent, he'd add, and wink to imply wartime romance. For me as a child, this seemed both thrilling, right out of James Bond, and deeply distressing, my father in love with a random woman while he was supposed to be defeating Nazis and missing his wife and small children at home. My mother saw it as performance, at least on the surface, and presumably so did their guests. She would sit at the other end of our long dining table, look at her husband across the candle glow as a maid cleared the dessert plates and poured one last round of wine, and say, "Oh god, there you go again," and roll her eyes. Yet I noticed the look that came over him as he sang those nights. His eyes got moist; he looked toward the window and his voice seemed almost to crack, as if for that instant it all fell away— the guests, the candlelight, the city noise below—and he was back in a world of international conflict, romance, and espionage, a world where by just "summoning up" a language, his words could cast magical spells.

One evening I found a great commotion in the square. A number of trucks had suddenly appeared with Italian partisans and they were about to batter down the doors of the German officer's building. A man who appeared to be in charge gave me to understand that they intended to lynch a certain German lieutenant who, they assured me, had been guilty of various war crimes. Summoning up my best Italian, I told the partisan leader that, although the Germans were still technically in charge of the town, authority had passed to the British and Americans and that we couldn't permit a bloodbath.

This is my father recounting his activities in the OSS at the close of the war in Europe. I heard him give the interview to a man named Russell Miller for his book *Behind the Lines* about the OSS. I was about ten, curled on the couch beside him as he spoke. I had arrived home after school, kicked off my shoes, and in my uniform wandered in to see my father in his best suit speaking to a man taking notes. He waved me in as he spoke, put a finger to his lips to ensure I stayed quiet, and as I curled up on the couch beside him he went on. It took me years to find the book in which the interview appeared. He speaks of controlling German and Italian and Allied troops like a nanny in a room of overtired children.

I sent one of our GIs, who happened to be in the neighborhood, back to our headquarters to summon help, moral, if not physical, and arranged that an American tank, also there by chance, should circle the square with the Stars and Stripes prominently displayed. Within a few minutes an American officer arrived who was of Italian descent and who had worked closely with the partisans. He was able to persuade them that no good would come of an Italian–German confrontation and that justice would, in the end, be served.

After that VE day itself was something of an anti-climax. We celebrated it with Champagne, which we had taken from the Germans, who had taken it from the French. In the midst of our party, a German major arrived, sat down casually at the piano and started playing Strauss waltzes. This was interrupted when an upper-class British officer gruffly declared that this was a "bad show" and "not at all the thing to do." It was left to me to explain to the German major that while we liked his music, this was neither the time nor the place for it.

His first wife waited years for his return, and finally found love elsewhere, something they all appeared to accept without acrimony, and when he returned home from the war to Washington, DC, they divorced. He then moved to New York and to projects as varied as editing a Latin American journal and working as a freelance journalist.

This is their story of how my parents met:

"We were at a cocktail party"—my father.
"We were at Sally Stamm's cocktail party, in her
*   garden"—my mother.*
"Somewhere uptown"—my father.
"On East 92nd Street, between Park and Lex"—my mother.
"We were immediately drawn to each other"—my father.
"Daddy had a 'tootsie' on his arm"—my mother.
Laughter from my father, hand goes to forehead in amused
*   exasperation.*
"Very tacky woman"—my mother.

"Honey, come on"—my father.

"Someone should have taken that monkey and put her back in her cage"—my mother.

"Honey, please. Anyhow. We were pleasantly conversing, and suddenly an ashtray came flying across the garden, narrowly missing us both"—my father.

"The tootsie was throwing it at me"—my mother.

"We never knew which of us she was throwing it at"—my father.

"I could tell, it was me"—my mother.

"So when it was time to leave, I asked Sally, 'Sally,' said I, 'who is that divine creature with whom I was just speaking?'"—my father.

"He took a year to call me"—my mother.

"That's right, I took a year"—my father.

"A full year"—my mother.

"You didn't want me to call while I was still seeing someone else, did you?"—my father.

"That tootsie. What you ever saw in that cheap girl I'll never know"—my mother.

"I was thinking about you every day in that year, Pat"—my father.

"He took a year to call me, he's lucky I hadn't run off with someone else"—my mother.

"I was very lucky indeed"—my father.

"A full year, girls, your father took a year to call me, a year almost to the day after his cheap tootsie threw an ashtray at my head"—my mother.

"I was trying to be a gentleman"—my father.

"I had a lot of other suitors"—my mother.
"It was the longest year I ever waited for anything, and that
includes waiting for the war to end"—my father.
"Jean-Jean"—my mother, pronouncing it in the French
manner.
"My darling dear"—my father.

In a black leather suitcase my father kept all the cards my mother had ever sent him. Each card is addressed to "Jean-Jean" and signed "Patsy Poo." In the suitcase, there are also envelopes with all our school report cards and our baby teeth. Teeth dating from my half siblings in the 1940s, all the way up to my sister Catherine's teeth in the mid-'60s. He put the teeth in plain white envelopes and marked the date, with the age of each child. There were far fewer from the half siblings, as he saw them so infrequently a tooth loss was no doubt rare on those visits. Still they are all stored there in his suitcase. Twenty years' worth of baby teeth shed by his children. In large manila envelopes, there were love letters from women all over Europe in various languages, professing undying passion in the time of wartime pandemonium. These were mixed in among the teeth and report cards. "I know you are probably back Stateside by now," one woman named Susan wrote, "with your wife and children, and I hope your life will go on happily. As for me, I will never again be as happy as when we were together . . ." There were war journals written in his almost illegible scrawl. "I dreamed I was on a train going through high mountains," one entry said, written in 1942. "I couldn't get off and the train wouldn't stop."

For my father, when he met my mother, there was no apparent shame in not making a salary. And despite her concerns voiced at the ladies' lunch at Gino's, she seemed to take to the life he could afford, and together they moved to an apartment high above Park Avenue shortly before I was born. My father's day-to-day reality was to sit in our living room all morning in his bathrobe, with a book in his hand and stacks of index cards in piles by his feet, filling the cards with words in whatever language he was studying that year. Verb declensions scattered all over my mother's soft dove-gray rug. At noon, he'd take a shower and put on a suit. He always wore a dark suit, with a white shirt and a blue tie. "It brings out the blue in his eyes," my mother would say of his collection of blue silk ties. He never left our apartment building in anything but a jacket and tie—he was proud of mentioning that the doorman had never seen him any other way. This included during the elevator strike when he did his shift taking residents up and down the building in his suit. Once dressed for lunch, he would walk the short distance to Café Geiger on East 86th Street, or down to Lüchow's on Union Square, so he could keep up his German over assorted wurst or corned pork knuckle with sauerkraut. His trajectory midday in the city was so predictable that when years later I got my acceptance to college, I knew to call Café Geiger and have the maître d', a dear friend of my father's by this point, put him on the phone.

After lunch, my father rode in taxis. He would hail a cab to take him home, always with the hope that he'd wind up in a cab with a driver who spoke a language that interested him. In that case his afternoon plan was cemented, and he'd have them drive, no particular destination in mind, so he could practice whatever language the driver spoke. He'd strike up conversations in Urdu or Serbo-Croatian or Hungarian or Greek or Spanish or French or any of another handful of languages, making small talk well into the afternoon if he found the conversation too important to abandon. As he sent the cab on long lazy circumambulations around Central Park, he asked questions ("How did you come by your English, my good man, was it in grade school or when you arrived on our shores? Tell me, how do you view Americans as a rule? What do they say back home in your country about our president? Say, are you raising your children here in New York? Bilingually? You must, it's the finest gift a child can receive.").

Late afternoons, my father arrived home just as we'd be returning from school and after homework we'd sit with him in the library and watch television—*I Love Lucy* or *Gilligan's Island* or the bewildering *Dark Shadows*. He'd occasionally let us take out his comb and we'd style his hair up in puffs on top of his head as we watched television. When my mother happened upon us, she'd find three girls in their school tunics and stocking feet, her husband in a smoking jacket with his hair up in puffs on top of his head and the TV set on. He'd have his first scotch of the evening on the coffee table, the ice cubes melting. His favorite was *I Love Lucy*, and he laughed a high-pitched giggle as Lucy and Ethel got into household capers, flooding the house with soapsuds or picking chocolates off a conveyer belt. The quiet snarl of Dewar's scotch was there with us too. Faint but pervasive. Into the evening hours it lingered. Scotch as we grew up became not a substance at all but a characteristic. Scotch was my father, his smell.

He became president of an organization called the English-Speaking Union, and under those auspices my father founded, published, and edited a monthly newsletter called *English Around the World*. He featured monthly articles on topics that included "Inbreeding and the Aboriginal Subjunctive" and "Togo's Many Dialects." These were the concerns that drove his passions, the demise of the subjunctive form among the descendants of Northern Finns in Australia or the evolution of dialects in Togo. Once a week he and my mother had a secretary, Mrs. Bertcher, come and sit in the living room at a folding bridge table near my father's chair in the mornings. On the street below there would be the daily sound of jackhammers fracturing the smooth sidewalks of the Upper East Side, pavement that in the sunshine glinted like mirrors up and down the avenues. Amid the clang of the workday breaking in small dramas around the neighborhood, Mrs. Bertcher would ride the elevator to the eighteenth floor, hang her coat in the closet off the foyer, unfold the bridge table and chair, unlock the typewriter she stored in a hard leather carrying case, and settle in for the morning, taking dictation from a man in his pajamas and slippers as he edited his newsletter for his beloved English-Speaking Union—the ESU, as he called it. My mother also had need of Mrs. Bertcher from time to time, to make social engagements or type letters, and Mrs. Bertcher would go from the living room to the library, where my mother sat every morning on her side of the couch. There she'd perch on the edge of a leather wingback chair and take notes on a yellow legal pad. My parents both called her "Bertcher" as if it were her secret agent name—"Have Bertcher take care of it," they'd say to each other, or "Get Bertcher in ASAP," or "This is a job for Bertcher."

It also fell to Mrs. Bertcher to type up the Franklin stories.

For years, my father had been working on the Franklin stories, a series of stories for my sisters and me, at my urging. Knowing his handwriting was impossible, he wrote them as they came to him, and then later dictated the stories to Mrs. Bertcher in his pajamas. His alter ego was an octopus named Franklin. The stories were Franklin's bar stories, the people he met as he lounged at his favorite bar, which my father had named Ralph's Rest. The significant thing about Franklin was that, being an octopus, he would order eight scotches at one time, one for each arm. Sometimes, he would ask Ralph to make it a double or a triple. Scotches in the story multiplied by eight.

When my father wasn't at home studying languages, index cards at his feet, he took us traveling where he could use them.

The summer we were in Greece, he taught us how to write the Greek alphabet. He propped up his books on the table in the hotel suite, open at the spine, so we could follow along. He always traveled with boxes of No. 2 pencils, sharp and new, and gave us each a pencil and a package of unopened index cards, still fresh in their cellophane wrapping. He had whole suitcases just for supplies such as these, language books, pencils, and index cards. When my family traveled, my sisters and I had one suitcase each, my mother had an enormous folding Val-A-Pak, and my father had six suitcases mottled with luggage tags.

"I'll teach you a word," he'd say. "'*Parakalo*.' You can use it at dinner tonight. It means 'please.' Then you say, '*Efcharisto*'—'thank you.' '*Efcharisto poly*'—'thank you very much'—if you want to be extra polite."

"*Efcharisto poly*."

"Good. If you write it down on an index card, I'll check your lettering."

My sisters and I spent vacation hours in hotel suites writing vocabulary words on index cards in new languages. If we were well behaved in restaurants, he promised to bark like a seal at the waiter when he came by with the check. We held up our end of the bargain and so did he. "Thank you very much," he'd say to the waiter, then pretend to reach for his wallet, pause, and look up at the waiter and open his mouth as if to ask a question. Instead, he'd let out a loud series of barks, startling many a waiter and surrounding tables of guests. "I gave him a good tip," he'd say as we'd leave the restaurant. "Affable fellow."

Our laughter, he said, was everything. Ditto, I might say to that. His laugh was the freest thing about him.

"Laughter is the universal language," he used to tell us. "The great unifier. Never forget that."

A photograph has the date June 1965 stamped on the white-rimmed edge of the print. We are at the Parthenon, running along the sun-bleached slabs of limestone, playing hide-and-seek. My two sisters and I are dressed in matching sundresses and white Mary Janes; my father is in a short-sleeved white shirt and gray lightweight suit trousers. He would be counting out loud to ten in Greek while we hid. In the picture, we are behind him, peeking out from behind the marble columns. He stands on the stones of the ancient Greek acropolis with his light blue sports jacket draped over his head, so as not to peek as he called out the numbers: *"Ena, dio, tria, tessera, pente, exi, efta, octo, ennea, deka!"*

. . .

"How do you say 'lion' in Swahili?" we asked one summer when we were in Kenya. We were driving through the arid country-side. Occasionally we'd pass elephants and okapi and warthogs along the way. We wanted to see a lion.

"'*Simba*.' Say '*sim-ba*.' Go ahead, try it."

Often, on long road trips, our parents sang. My father had an easy tenor voice, my mother, though she couldn't hold a tune, sang with a playful, rhythmic exuberance.

Together they sang duets, love songs, show tunes. "You're Not Sick, You're Just in Love" was a favorite. My father crooned. My mother snapped her fingers as she sang a jaunty accompaniment.

We were on our way from Nairobi to a Masai village so my father could practice his Swahili. I wonder what they must have thought of us, the regal Masai villagers, their bright cloths wrapped around them, when we emerged from our rented van. Our van was white with black zebra stripes, as were all the vans rented to tourists. My mother had gone to Abercrombie & Fitch on Madison Avenue before the trip and outfitted herself and my father in khaki outdoor wear, which the Abercrom-bie catalogue referred to as "Safari Chic." While she poked out from the sunroof of the van with her camera, my father emerged with Pam, our British guide, and engaged in lengthy though halting conversation with a tall Masai tribesman. The man wore a lush orange cotton wrap and nodded as my father spoke. Soon both my father and the Masai were laughing their heads off.

My father had three rules for measuring proficiency in a language. Can you tell a joke, can you understand song lyrics, and finally, do you ever dream in that language? The last, the dreaming, was the final test of proficiency. "But start with the joke," he'd remind us. "If you can tell a joke in a foreign language, you reach across cultures, time zones, and barriers you girls can't possibly realize. It's the unifier, I always tell you girls that. You make a lot of friends through laughter."

By the time we went to Africa, I was thirteen and our traveling road show embarrassed me. My mother dressed up like Katharine Hepburn in *The African Queen*, her noisy Super 8 movie camera going out the top of the sunroof, we three girls in the back seat of the zebra van, my father busting into the Masai's daily routine to tell a few jokes, as if he were some kind of freelance Bob Hope. What I remember of that day is a woman holding a tiny baby wrapped tight about her chest in a carrier made of bright pink-and-green fabric. She wore long strands of beads in many colors. She had the tired, patient face of an overwhelmed young mother. Beside her, a young boy, a boy around eight, the age of my sister Catherine, was crying, his ankle tied to a pole by thin rope.

"That fellow was a very amusing chap," my father said of his new Masai friend when we were settled in the car and driving back to Nairobi. "Good sport letting me barge in on him like that." He laughed to himself as we drove along the dry dirt roads.

"What did he do, the kid?" we wanted to know. We wouldn't let this go and kept asking our father all the way back to Nairobi. "Why did they tie him up?"

"Honey, that's their culture, not ours." He pulled out the phrasebook and passed it back. "'*Samahani*,' say."

"*Samahani*."

"That's right. *Samahani*." He sighed. "It means 'I'm sorry.'

I think he had probably done something naughty, and she was waiting for him to apologize."

"*Samahani*," we repeated.

"As much as you should say 'please' and 'thank you' in each language, 'I'm sorry' is pretty useful too, if you get into scrapes," he told us as we drove.

"Which John McCulloch never does, does he?" my mother said from the front of the van.

"Me? Honey. Scrapes? I never."

"I'll be the judge of that," she said. Sometimes, the mood between them altered suddenly.

The truth was, he did get into scrapes. He would go off "exploring," as he called it, in cities we visited and return late and sloppy. Sometimes his traveler's checks or watch went missing during these excursions, and like a tarnished angel he wanted forgiveness. In these instances, for long empty hours his remorse hung heavily in the air, gray and loud, drowning out any other family life. He'd shuffle around or sit silent in a chair in our hotel suite, watching us but not seeing us, his eyes watery, his body hunched, a man slumped in guilt. And then he would drink more, another scotch or another martini. He'd hold the glass in his hand and tears would run down his cheeks. As a child, it was painful and terrifying to watch this man, our sweet and loving father who spoke volumes in a multitude of tongues, who barked like a seal for our amusement, now changed horribly in the space of a few hours into a well of helplessness, and self-pity.

It was the remorse of the alcoholic. For years I thought of his demeanor in these episodes as pathetic and it made me angry. Yet being only a child, I blamed myself for my anger—it seemed wrong somehow, to feel irritation.

My mother, impatient, seethed. Rows in hotel suites were a feature of these trips, and the pattern tinged our childhood. We did not know when our playful father would disappear behind his eyes and a blundering facsimile take his place. Not knowing when the cycle would recur scared us. As we got older, the cycle was more frequent, and as he got older, the cycle was more severe. I was young though, and I didn't see it as a feature of having an alcoholic parent. I just reacted to the familiar pattern the same way every time: He "was bad" and in his subsequent guilt he inspired anger, then pity. My mother lashed out and we felt angry at her for yelling and angry at him for being pathetic. We'd retreat. The child of an alcoholic retreats in many ways; the subtlest is the retreat into the background, into silence. I recognized it only as self-preservation at the time, but of course it was self-abnegation, a hardscrabble strategy that becomes the automatic response to trauma, the desire to disappear.

Then there was the physical retreat. The need to be anywhere but where the episode was unraveling. When we were home, we could simply retreat into our rooms, but in the hotel episodes, retreat was nearly impossible. Being too young to be allowed outside by ourselves in those early years, we developed elaborate escapes within hotel confines, plotting elevator races through the hotel to escape the din. The rules would be devised on the spot and someone would yell "Go!": run to the eighth floor, pass through the whole hallway front to back once, then take the elevator to three, run down to the lobby, past the ladies having tea, take the elevator down to the Grill Room floor below, then up to the lobby, touch the concierge desk, then back to our door. By the time we'd run down the long carpeted halls that smelled like perfume, past the women in furs drinking tea in the lobby amid the ferns, and back up to our door, we'd be breathless and invigorated. We'd return to our rooms laughing, the silence no longer deafening. Our father would have gone to sleep or would be watching television with a blank stare. Our mother would be waiting. Sometimes we'd go with her for a walk outside, the fresh air bracing. She knew we needed an out, and hotel managers were handsomely tipped, I imagine, to indulge our relay drills. Casing hotels for potential elevator-race tracks was always something we did when we arrived. We had to be prepared. We never knew when it would all happen again, but it always did.

Outside, that day in the zebra-striped van, the sun blasted the baked African plains, and herds of giraffes walked languidly in the tall yellow grass, their necks slanted forward as if leaning into the windless afternoon. These days held a golden extravagance wreathed in an intangible tension, which was often my memory of trips with my father in pursuit of words. By the time I was in college I had stopped traveling with my family altogether. I thought if I stopped and stayed home, then instead of retreating I'd actually be moving forward, like those giraffes that appeared to be leaning into the future as they made their way through the midday heat. I'd make my own way, and the reminder of our family sorrow would leave town without me and for a while I'd be whole.

These are the naive expectations brought about by a blind faith, as if there were shortcuts to our wholeness and to my father's redemption. Blind in the belief that things would change. Life could only go back to where it had been upon their return.

. . .

I believe words danced in my father's head. Even as he sat in our living room in his bathrobe, index cards by his feet and the morning can of Budweiser on a tray at his side, words were his passport to a world far outside his imagination. Words were his power.

Danish was his final language. He was translating a novel from Danish into English the summer he died, and the index cards by his feet the last time I spoke to him were Danish words he collected as he worked on the translation.

Pearls of wisdom, he said, each word is a pearl of wisdom, and in the art of translation you recognize you cannot replicate a pearl, yet you are called to equal its luster in the passage. That is the art. That is the challenge. Pearls of wisdom. Translation is a calling.

> *My father: "Respect the words, girls. They will open doors to you that you've never imagined."*
> *My mother: "Respect the sea, girls. It can turn on you in an instant."*

These are the lessons we learned as children.

Full fathom five thy father lies . . .
Those are pearls that were his eyes.

· V ·

The Perilous Dune

WHEN I WAS young, before I was old enough to lie about where I'd been the night before or how late I'd come home, the thing I lied about with frequency was my address. Not egregiously, but artfully. I would say when asked that I lived between Madison and Park Avenues on 73rd Street in Manhattan, which, if one determined our address from the fact that our apartment was in the rear elevator bank of the building, would have been correct. Our kitchen, eighteen stories up, overlooked the courtyard, so why not claim it as my address? Nothing could have gotten me to admit to a stranger that in fact the entrance to the building was around the corner on Park Avenue, and that my family resided for twenty-five years in the duplex at the top. I was too wary of what the immediate calculation would be. Money. That inherited wealth could be a birthright, a genetic twist of fate as random as, say, red hair or a predisposition to drink, was a notion I distrusted. How much was real, and how much was illusion, and how might the perception of money make any one person different from anyone else? These were questions I pondered uneasily as a child as I lied about my address.

On the left-leaning side of Manhattan in the late '60s and early '70s when I grew up, the political maelstrom gave birth to the "limousine liberal," a breed of which my mother was a charter member. When I think of my mother in that era, by day she is disappearing into a hired black limousine, her Hermès scarf tied neatly over her head, off to tutor young children in an East Harlem storefront. My father went about his day, settling into his world of words and ideas and index cards. By night, he gamely donned his tuxedo whenever my mother declared it was time for a party. Which, very often, she did. As a child, I recognized that the smell of Chanel perfume in the hallway leading to the master bedroom meant a night on the town. I would knot my father's bow tie and help push the ebony studs into his dress shirt. He would pat a cigar into the pocket of his coat. My mother wore long feathered ball gowns with a string of emeralds around her neck, and after she left, my sisters and I would collect the stray feathers that had fallen on the rug. Sometimes as I fell asleep I'd picture my parents waltzing, moving together with such grace and synchronicity it seemed they'd been dancing together forever, as indeed, in my mind, they had.

In our family, as in many families, we put on black armbands and marched to save the planet, end the war, end poverty; we marched for civil rights and women's rights; we leafleted, picketed, rode buses to Washington, DC, to scream our heads off, yet when all was said and done, and everyone was off the bus, back in the gilded ballrooms of Manhattan, in true Gatsbyesque fashion, the band played on—the crystal glasses clinked, the candles glowed, and under majestic chandeliers, the hems of elaborate dresses swished along marble dance floors.

My father bought the house in East Hampton when my sisters and I were young because, he said—despite his endless pilgrimages in search of, say, a Masai tribesman to speak Swahili with or a Kashmiri taxi driver to chat with in Urdu or a Scottish bartender with whom to shoot the shit in Gaelic—he wanted us always to have a family home. So that by shaping sand into castles, spitting watermelon seeds down one another's shirts, and surf-casting for blues and stripers every Labor Day, we might put down roots.

So that we would be a family.

Most summer evenings we children ate a rushed, chaotic dinner early, in an airy avocado-green parlor just off the kitchen, eager to bolt back outside before dark, while the sky was lavender and the sand on the beach still warm from the day's sun. On the last night of every summer, when we younger ones were invited to eat with the adults, the dark wood table in the dining room would be stretched to full length to seat twenty-six with all the leaves slotted in. The extra-long damask tablecloth used for special occasions would be smoothed down, the best china and goblets set. My mother stood by her chair at the head of the table and seated us one by one around the table. At the meal's end, she made an annual toast to the "clan," as she called us, and from her seat at the head of the long table she'd hurl her wineglass over her shoulder so it shattered against the mantel in infinitesimal slivers of crystal, always just narrowly missing the oil painting of the nude woman above. It was a violent, passionate act that made me convinced that amid the finger bowls, the candlelight, against the soundtrack of the crashing waves, and in the tolerant, bemused presence of a uniformed butler named Fred, perhaps we were all slightly, if not totally, mad, and perhaps the cushion that wealth provided had made us so.

"We live on such a perilous dune," my mother would say as late-summer storm season approached. She would sit reading the *New York Times*, her half-glasses on her nose, scrutinizing the weather report as the wind blew in audible moans and the sea bounded up toward the house. She was a Florida girl, my mother, and to her, hurricanes meant you filled all the bathtubs with water, put batteries in the radio and the flashlights, lit candles, opened wine, and ate everything in the freezer. "We live on such a perilous dune," she'd say. "All of this could just go"—and she'd snap her fingers—"like that."

As a child, I was haunted by images of the hurricane of 1938, shaky black-and-white film reels, shown occasionally on the television, of entire families on the roofs of their homes, as thunderous waves came and washed them out to sea. I pictured us all: a giant ark, a floating mansion, drifting helplessly out to sea, scrambling for something to save.

We live on such a perilous dune. All of this could just go, like that.

So money, what of it? A long gray shingled house by the sea, a bonfire lighting up the night sky on summer evenings, a softly lit tent where guests danced in late summer—does the

postcard beauty of those scenes suggest that beautiful times
were more beautiful for my family than for others, or terrible
times more terrible? Our lives might have looked pretty because the backdrop looked pretty. Certainly, it might be less
inspiring of empathy than of cynicism. It might be all those
things, and that's fair to assume. But like alcoholism, despair is
an equal-opportunity condition, and the daily human struggle
to escape its grip knows no boundaries of wealth or class. One
of my earliest memories is when one of our neighbors left his
own beautiful house and swam into the sea because he didn't
love his life despite his beautiful wife and his beautiful kids and
his beautiful bank account. As the Coast Guard dragged his
body out of the surf in front of our house, in front of our eyes,
he wept that he had been saved, then swam out again and again
until later that summer he finally swam out for keeps.

"He was blue," I heard Laura, the housekeeper, tell Johanna
in the kitchen, "when they finally dragged the body out."

"It took hours for the body to wash ashore," Vincent, our
gardener, added. The household staff were all congregated in
the kitchen discussing it while in the parlor we children sat at
dinner, pushing the food around, imagining Mr. Crawford's
dead body rolling in the waves.

"I saw him," my cousin Pierre told us as we ate. "He was
blue, and, and his belly was bloated out.

"His eyes were open," Pierre added. "Like, all bugged out."

I imagined Mr. Crawford's eyes like marbles.

Early on I understood that a mansion by the sea can just as
easily be a jail cell as a dreamscape.

· VI ·

The Protocol of the Toast

"I DON'T KNOW why that Ruth Ann Middleton has to put her sticky finger in everything."

"You hired her, Ma. Her finger is in everything because you hired it to be."

"There is an order to things, and Ruth Ann Middleton isn't calling this one. I'm calling this one, dearie."

The week before my wedding to Dean, my mother was complaining about the protocol of wedding toasts. The rule my mother wanted followed was that toasts are only made the night before the wedding, never at the reception. This ended up not being one of Ruth Ann's rules. Worse, Ruth Ann went so far as to tell my mother no one in the history of weddings had ever heard of the rule my mother wanted followed. Then she said the one thing that would be guaranteed to set my mother on edge.

"Pat," she had explained, "it simply isn't done."

· · ·

"Ruth Ann doesn't tell me what is and what isn't done. I am the mother of the bride. This is my wedding."

"Technically, it's mine."

"What's yours."

"The wedding is technically mine. Mine and Dean's."

"It can be yours all you want when you pay for it. Your second wedding can be your wedding, because you're not getting a second one out of me. This one is mine." Then she corrected herself, "Daddy's and mine."

This conversation took place a week before the wedding as she stood on the small deck outside her bedroom, deadheading the row of pink geraniums planted in boxes along the perimeter. She worked methodically as she spoke, snapping the dried old flowers off the green stems with her right hand and holding them in her left. "You must be a ruthless gardener to make a beautiful garden," she always said. She walked back through the French doors into her pink room, clutching the bouquet of dead flowers, and turned to her sister.

"You never, ever make a wedding toast after the wedding. Only the night before," my mother was saying to her sister. "We know that, don't we, Sissy?"

My aunt Jeanne, my beautiful quiet aunt, looked like she was the victim in a hostage crisis. She sat perched on the edge of a silk shantung chaise in the corner of my mother's bedroom. She had come up from her home in Florida a week before the wedding at my mother's request. My mother was using her as something of a human shield, insisting she be in place well before the Jacksons and her stepchildren, my half siblings, arrived.

She had a complex relationship with my aunt Jeanne. My aunt, three years older, lived in Coconut Grove, the same leafy section of Miami where they'd grown up. Aunt Jeanne had married a boy from upstate New York after graduating from Vassar, and settled back in Miami to raise five children. Aunt Jeanne walked on her tiptoes in bare feet. This was from years of wearing heels, but I felt it was also indicative of her demure character. Whereas my mother strode, my aunt tiptoed. Her house was always slightly rumpled and chaotic, but as the ceiling fans blew a soft breeze, she and her husband, my uncle Jooge, held hands and looked at each other like they had just met and fallen in love. This no doubt drove my mother crazy. The sisters had grown up in Miami back in the '20s and '30s, when it was a grove of grapefruit trees and shaded streets, the branches of the trees grown toward one another over the years to form a graceful canopy along the main residential road. In the 1920s, the adults took wood-sided boats into Biscayne Bay to have "chowder parties"—weekend outings that involved booze and soup. They dressed in white cotton suits and long lacy dresses and set off from the Key Biscayne Yacht Club with picnic hampers. The women carried delicate cotton parasols to protect against the Florida sun. My grandfather Simon Pierre Robineau was a Frenchman who had migrated to the area with his wife after attending Harvard Law School. An injury in World War I to his lung required a move to a warm climate, and at the time Miami was an area of vast opportunity for young lawyers. In photographs, his swooping black mustache and sallow features gave him a Proustian look of Gallic melancholy despite his robust American patriotism. I was named for my aunt Jeanne, and I had the impression early on I was somehow supposed to make up for what my mother saw as a lifetime of lost battles in sibling rivalry. "Our mother always liked Sissy better," my mother would say, adding as evidence, "She left all the family silver to Sissy." But she never stopped just there. In the next breath, it would be "Sissy inherited everything," and following that, "Sissy was the favorite child," and then, "Everyone liked Sissy best," spiraling finally into "No one cared about me." When she spoke like this, I pictured my mother as a little girl. Despite the foreign accents she employed to her use, it became clear to me early on that my mother's true voice, the voice deep inside her, was that of a hurt child. It was as if there was a hole in her soul, not in her heart but in her very soul, that no amount of grand gestures, family silver, Lilly Pulitzers and ball gowns, or the endless dappled vistas of our life was ever going to fill. In one more of her ongoing attempts at belated parity, she was making my aunt Jeanne give all the Robineau family silver to me, not to her own daughter but to me, as a wedding present—an exercise that made my aunt wistful and me abashed, and seemed to have put my mother temporarily at peace. She was like that, my aunt Jeanne; she gave in to my mother's dramatic demands, either out of guilt, perhaps, or because, her life being content, annoyingly content in my mother's mind, she gave my mother whatever would appease her for the moment. The two sisters spoke every day. Sunday evenings, the two finished the *New York Times* crossword puzzle together over the phone—my mother in her nightgown with her feet up on the coffee table, my aunt down in Miami on her veranda under the ceiling fan.

The toast conversation in my mother's bedroom took place while I was at the house for the weekend for a final run-through of the wedding to-do list with her. Downstairs in the sunroom, my father was bent over a yellow legal pad, a pencil in hand. As always, his glasses slid down his nose, and it being evening, he wore a maroon smoking jacket over a white button-down shirt, the shirt pulling slightly across his belly in between the buttons. I was returning to New York for a few days before the wedding, and went into the sunroom in the evening to find him there.

He looked at me over his reading glasses, the lenses thick and smudged. Though it was a gentle August evening, he was in his heavy smoking jacket. "I'm writing a toast for your wedding," he said. His hand shook, and the spider crawl of letters, always difficult to read, now seemed like rickety skeletons limping across the page. Some words were jagged and trailed off in places, as if he'd been writing fast in the back of a racing van in the dark.

"It's not much. But it's the best I can manage right now."

"The best I can manage right now" was often as modest a statement as "summoning up my best" French or German or Swahili or Yoruba or whatever, though this time he followed it with this, "After I give the toast, I'm going to drink. That's fair."

One thing about families. When secrets come out, they lie like long gray shadows over entire sections of life. My sisters, my aunt, and Dean and I knew what nobody else did, which was that before my father died, my mother had left him. Or at least kicked him to the side with an ultimatum, designed to jar him into realizing he could not keep up his drinking and stay married.

As he got older, my father's drinking affected more and more of his day, and with all her children out of the nest, my mother saw his increasing unreliability, often incoherence, as a weight she could no longer bear.

"I'm not abandoning him," she would say. "He abandoned me. A long time ago. Look at him."

Even as he sat beside her, he was no longer coherently there.

"You all abandoned me," she would go on to say to us, as if with an empty nest, our leaving her alone with a man in a stupor was a betrayal on some level.

They were selling our childhood apartment and moving to a smaller one up the street in September, following my wedding to Dean.

In early July, she lodged my father in the Carlton House on Madison Avenue, a residential hotel "where all the divorcés and widowers stay," she said, and ignoring her wedding planning and everyone involved a month before the date, she flew to a rented villa in Portugal with a few peripheral friends, leaving my father and Ruth Ann and the caterers and Dean and me and everyone else in limbo. To me it felt like she was trying to run for her life, or perhaps more accurately it was from her life that she was running. Judging from the speed and spontaneity of her departure, both appeared to be the case.

My father's apartment at the Carlton House when he got there in early July was just what I imagined a little apartment of his would look like: stacks of books and index cards all over the living room and front hall; bottles and bottles of Mylanta, aspirin, hair tonic, and toothpaste lining the bathroom sink and behind the toilet; his half-unpacked suitcases—dusty, mottled with decades of peeling luggage stickers—all over the bedroom floor. "They're building me bookshelves in September," he would say when we dropped by to visit, stepping through the mess.

Bookshelves in September meant something. It was a statement that had nothing to do with construction but with resolve. He had decided to drink. My mother had told him if he was sober, he could move back home, yet he was having the Carlton House build him bookshelves in September. He was choosing bookshelves over sobriety.

He never filled his kitchen because he never learned how to cook. It remained the one clean, untouched place in his apartment. Everything else was sprawl and muddle, but the kitchen always looked as though no one had ever moved in. When we visited, he'd order up cheese and crackers from room service, and we'd pick at it while we tried to fix things up: poking tentatively through old notebooks and papers to make piles, folding socks into tight balls, hanging pictures on the walls. In the bedroom, we put old family photographs: my parents on a road trip when they were courting, him up on the curb and her on the sidewalk so it appeared that he was taller, she in a gray suit, her hair curled up in a flip at her shoulders. We had others, the three of us after school sprawled on the couch watching television with him, one or the other of us having talked him into taking out his comb. In the photos, his hair stands on top of his head, our four faces lightly illuminated by the television's glow. In others, we're in matching dresses flanking our father in a park. In those days, my father was still thin and his smile still broad and radiant as he held our hands.

When my father looked at our pictures, we waited for him to say something big, something with a sigh, but he didn't. He'd turn and say, "Who in this room is for going out to dinner?"

By the end of our evenings together, when we were all drowsy from summer humidity and wine, he often spoke of our mother, calling her "your mother," as though she were already a distant speck in his mind.

It was one of the last days of July, when it's like moving through cushions, the streets of New York close and thick, that I saw him on the street. Well, glimpsed, really. I was riding a bus up Madison Avenue in the dusk. The bus stopped at a light near the Carlton House, and out the window I saw him walking slowly down the sidewalk. He was dressed in his usual suit and blue tie, and I wondered how despite his disorientation he managed to dress himself up and stay true to his belief that in New York City, it was important to always wear a suit outdoors. Aged pale as milk, he moved in small steps with his fists up in knots, his head bowed low to the pavement. I thought to get out, to ask him if I could take him home, to ask him how I could help. But instead I listened to the offhand mumble and chat of the bus passengers and the blare of the street. Then the light changed and my bus took off, leaving him walking down 63rd Street. I knew then that no matter what else ever happened, I'd see my father making his way down that side street forever.

When on the last day of July my mother returned from Portugal, tanned and sleek, with presents, she called us all and said, "Come for dinner, your father is coming over too, I'm sending a car for him."

He was pasty after a month at the Carlton House without her, and could hardly hold his head up. He slumped on his side of their couch, his mouth agape. She looked at him, and looked at the lists and lists of wedding details she'd spread out on the coffee table, and issued an ultimatum. "Look," she told us, speaking about him as if he were not in the room, as if he were not on his side of their shared couch. "Either he stops drinking, right here and now, or he is not welcome at the wedding."

He looked up as she said this. With my hand clenched in the armchair beside him, I dug my nails into my palm. "Honey," he said, and then some words, mumbles really, no one understood. His head went back on his chest, and he appeared to pass out sitting up.

"You kids go on home," she told us, ringing the bell for the elevator. "I'll get him into bed in his old room. I'll handle this."

The following day she took him out to East Hampton and began her own enforced dry-out strategy with no medical supervision. Looking back, I can't fathom why she did this without a proper detox protocol, except that maybe she didn't know of that necessity, or she felt she simply knew best. It would have been like her to think she knew best. In her defense, I would say that maybe she was trying to save him the only way she knew how.

In the kitchen, Johanna loaded fruits and vegetables into the blender following instructions my mother had carefully written out on a yellow legal pad in green ink. The recipes for "health shakes" came from a book called *Thirty Days to a Healthier You* that my mother had found in the local bookstore. "Your poor daddy," Johanna would say in her Irish brogue. "Saints in heaven, bless this poor man having to drink these concoctions."

In the mornings and then again at dusk, Vincent walked my father up and down the driveway at my mother's request. In the flat glare of late-morning summer light and then in the lavender twilight, holding Vincent's arm, my father stepped slowly, teetering from side to side as if balancing, not walking, his legs brittle. Together the two men progressed slowly, Vincent in canvas work trousers and a denim shirt, my father in his smoking jacket. Step by step they made their way down the long gravel driveway and around the border of the property. Upstairs in the house my mother would be on her pink princess phone, seated on her bed, with lists and calendars. She'd speak with Ruth Ann, discussing the final wedding details, or with her sister and Bertcher, the secretary, to book her sister's travel plans to arrive urgently, earlier than planned, or with my sisters and me, reassuring us that everything was proceeding nicely and our father was "getting better every day" under her care. Meanwhile, the home my father had bought years earlier, to create a sense of family safety, family identity, he now shakily patrolled in the stark August light of morning and in the fading light at dusk. At age seventy-four, he was little more than a trespasser on the outer edges of that long-ago dream.

Quinta de Crianças Brincar. House of Playing Children.
Children at Play.

By the time of our conversation in the sunroom, he had been off alcohol for a week. "I have such great hopes for you, for your life. I promised not to drink until after the wedding, and I won't. But right after, I will. That's fair."

Try to be fair, he had always told us. The world might not be fair, but you be fair.

I wanted to say something in the sunroom that evening, something that would keep him there.

Much as I couldn't get off the bus to stop him on Madison Avenue weeks earlier, I could not summon a voice he would hear. Perhaps I didn't know what I could possibly say. Even as an adult, the child of an alcoholic forgets how to speak; or, more accurately, loses the belief that their words have any power to make a difference or to matter. It was part of the strategy of retreat that we learned early in childhood to master. My father was a genius of language, but in the fog of his alcoholism, we all lost the power of impactful speech, the gift of communication. And anyway, I thought, he isn't here. He's long gone. He had disappeared behind his eyes. Disappeared somewhere cloudy and forever, somewhere no one could reach.

His voice grew soft, and he knew he was speaking the words that would disappoint. "I'm an old dog, honey," he told me. "No new tricks."

It was very still in the sunroom just then, just the sound of two people being quiet together, and the scratch of the fir tree's needles on the picture window in the dusk. And I knew that he was already gone.

· VII ·

The LIE

ON THE RADIO in the summer of 1983, Michael Jackson's "Billie Jean" topped the charts, along with the Police, "Every Breath You Take."

Two days before the wedding, Smokey Robinson was singing "Cruisin'" on the radio as Dean and I made our way out of town through the Midtown Tunnel.

In the back of our car we had my wedding dress in a garment bag, plus a duffle bag with two small blue Tiffany boxes, a single gold wedding band in each, and two slightly larger blue boxes with presents for the bridesmaids: a single pearl on a delicate gold chain, just short enough to allow the pearl to sit in the nape of the neck. Both of my sisters wore the necklaces the rest of the long week ahead. I remember looking at them several times during those days, remembering back to when we were in the car, wedding items in the back seat and the radio on. I remember Catherine fiddling with hers unconsciously, day after day, and thinking she should be careful not to break the delicate chain.

The road was mostly empty late morning on a Thursday in mid-August. Occasional trucks passed, making mid-island deliveries. The Long Island Expressway often had the reputation, in those days before HOV lanes were put in, of being "the world's largest parking lot," and so Dean and I left for East Hampton early. At any given stretch in the LIE, usually mid-island, the parking lot effect came into play: an accident or commuters or beachgoers—it all clogged the road, and hours would be added to the trip. Dean and I were both in a hurry and not that morning as we headed toward our wedding. As we loaded up the car, the trunk open, the radio already playing, it felt much the same as any other trip to visit my parents in East Hampton. We worked almost in silence, attending to details— wedding dress, suitcases with clothes for our honeymoon in Italy, the rings, and the presents for the bridesmaids. As we got closer to the Jones Beach exit, there were signs of holiday traffic, pickup trucks with surfboards piled in the back, convertibles filled with teenagers in sunglasses. And at that point the car slowed to a crawl.

"So now we're fucked," I said.

Dean laughed, his eyes on the road. He was like that; he didn't get rattled easily.

"Don't you think it's ironic," I said, "that no one ever comments on the fact that when you say 'LIE,' referring to the Long Island Expressway, what you're really spelling out is the word 'lie'?"

We were inching along behind a blue VW bus with bicycles strapped to the back and surfboards tied on the roof. "How do you boggle your brain like that," he said. "It just amazes me. What's going on in there?"

"No, I mean think about it. Just that as you hear the traffic reporter tell you, as we heard on the radio a few minutes ago, that 'traffic is running on or close to normal,' you promptly get snagged in a major rat fuck of a jam, you know? So, in essence, what you just heard on the radio about the LIE was in fact an l-i-e."

"A lie."

"Precisely." I held my arm out the window and cupped the warm humid August air in my palm as we passed the Jones Beach exit and gradually picked up speed again. "Lies, lies, lies. Far as the eye can see. This entire stretch is paved in lies. In each of the houses off every exit, people are telling lies. In every house, I bet there is at least one lie told a day."

Dean and I lived in a tiny ground-floor apartment on Horatio Street in the Far West Village, with a super who thought spacemen were speaking to him through the faucet in our bathroom. We had a small garden and a fireplace and a bedroom where a full-size bed filled the entire space. By day, Dean fed mice in a lab and took notes on their memory function. I had my first editorial job, as an assistant to the features editor at *Vogue* magazine in Midtown, a place where toned women editors clacked designer heels down smooth white corridors under harsh fluorescent lights.

Nights, I curled around Dean, or he around me. Our bodies fit perfectly together as we held each other through the night. Whatever else about us might not have fit perfectly—our life's ambitions, our priorities, our values—we assumed that those too gradually would evolve and softly form around each other's contours as well. I felt this was the protocol of love: you start in a safe embrace, and then that evolution as a couple, that growing to each other's contours, followed in time. You had to start somewhere. We were together, we were safe. The rest, we trusted, was bound to happen.

At exit 70 in Manorville, we stopped for gas and called the house from the pay phone to say we were running late. Dean had his hand in a bag of potato chips, the phone in the crook of his neck, when he suddenly stood straight and handed the phone to me. My mother's housekeeper spoke to me using my baby name. "JJ," she said, "keep driving straight to Southampton Hospital. Your daddy's had a stroke."

"A what?"

"A stroke," she repeated.

"I can't hear you, a what?"

"Your mother is there," she continued. "She said, if you called, to tell you to hurry up."

Just that morning, probably as Dean and I were leaving our apartment in the city, probably when Helen was laying her clothes on her bed and Raymond was securing the ribbons on the canoe, my mother, already in her tennis whites for the morning, found my father unconscious in his bed. She rode along in the back of the ambulance, down the sloping lawn, past the tent that was just that morning being erected, past the gardener making even lines as he mowed the grass, past the wild honeysuckle, past the cottage where the future in-laws would be housed, and past her driveway sign, "Drive Cautiously/Children at Play." The sirens wailed as they turned onto the main road. Wearing her pleated tennis skirt, the wedding preparations in full swing on the lawn as they passed, my mother sat helplessly, watching my father's labored breaths behind the oxygen mask that covered his face.

When Dean and I entered the hospital, we came upon my mother, as one would upon a familiar face at an airport, sitting in her outfit in the ER waiting room. A young doctor in green scrubs sat speaking with her in hushed tones, a clipboard on his lap.

"Well, *there* they are," she said, pointing at us, and the entire waiting room of the ER looked in our direction expectantly, as if we'd either done something wrong or brought the pizza they'd called out for. There was a mother with a crying child, two men in baseball caps, one holding a towel around his hand, an older couple holding hands, a few more people either sneezing, or bleeding, or whimpering, or reading, victims of minor colds and mishaps on a summer weekday. My mother swept her hand across the room to the assembled. "These are our lovebirds," she announced.

The doctor looked impassively at me. "I understand you're to be married on Saturday," he said, and nodded, perhaps a cue for us to do the same.

"In two days," my mother added to everyone in the room.

It was clear the doctor was used to giving people unwelcome information; he nodded and we nodded and he invited us into a private room. He pulled a shade down over the window on the door after he closed it shut.

"So, let me be candid with you, Jeanne." He pronounced it like "Gene."

My mother went into her French accent. "It's 'Jeanne,'" she said. "Jeanne *Robineau*, like Jeanne Moreau. Not Gene. *Jeanne.*

More like the *a* in the word 'man.'" She pronounced it as she always did: "*mahhhn.*" "My family is a French family."

"Whatever," I said. "Call me whatever. What's happening?"

"She hates us for giving her that name, but it's a beautiful name, she's named for my sister. Her aunt Jeanne. And her father cares very deeply, as do I, that she not go through life being called Gene or, worse, Genie, like she came out of a bottle."

"Mother, I don't care if he calls me an elephant's whore," I said. "What's going on?"

"Your father has suffered a massive stroke," he said. "There is no telling now if he'll make it or not. It could be tomorrow, it could be six months from now." He shrugged. "We can't be sure of anything. But it's serious."

"Well," my mother said, "the only thing we are sure of"— and she clenched her hand around mine—"is that there is going to be a wedding at our house this weekend. This is my baby girl. We have to get these two kids married. Isn't that right, Doctor?"

The doctor looked up from his clipboard. He thought for a moment.

"All I can say, not knowing your father, but being a new one myself, is that I'm sure he'd want you to go ahead with your plans for your wedding this weekend," he said. "It's supposed to be beautiful weather." To my mother he said, "A terrific day."

"Well, we took our chances, didn't we," she said, looking at me. "I mean, August can be hurricane season. But," she added, "I was raised in hurricanes. Nothing scares me." She flicked her hand. "Anyway, we have to get these kids married. That's all I care about."

"This is supposed to be a decent year, actually," the doctor said. "Not much chance of a turbulent season, hurricane-wise." And he walked off with his clipboard to make plans to transfer my father to the ICU.

"Well, I'll tell you kids one thing," my mother said as we drove home along Route 27 from the hospital. "First of all, that doctor didn't look old enough to be a father, did he. He didn't even look old enough to be a doctor."

"Let's hope he is one," Dean said.

"Second, luck is on our side," my mother continued. "First, I found Daddy this morning in time. That man could have been dead." She thought about that for a minute before adding with a sigh, "Good god, dearie, your father could have been dead. Can you imagine. After all this planning." Then she resumed. "Okay, back to the project at hand. We're damn lucky your brother Keith already rented a morning suit. If you hadn't asked him to be an usher, he wouldn't have it, and now he's really, really going to need it, I can tell you. He's going to have to walk you down the aisle. I know you wavered about imposing on him to be in the wedding party, but thank god you did. Kids, I think we can call that a blessing in disguise."

The usual roadside landmarks rushed by as we drove. The windmill by the Penny Candy Shop in Water Mill, the Bridgehampton drive-in, the driving range in Sagaponack, the Seafood Shop in Wainscott. After a time, my mother let out another long sigh. "Oh, my," she said, "your father's really gone and done it this time." She sat in the front seat, next to Dean. I sat in the back, next to my wedding dress. "I'm going to call the rest of the clan as soon as we get back to the house and tell them what's going on. This is now officially an emergency."

"Everyone's already on their way, Ma," I reminded her.

"And thank god for that. That's another blessing in disguise. We're lucky about a lot of things here today, all things considered."

As we got out of the car, we stood in the driveway. The party tent was up, and beside it the sprinklers misted the air in graceful arcs, making rainbows as the sunlight caught the spray.

This is now officially an emergency, I was thinking. *My wedding is officially an emergency.*

Out on the road just then there was a racket. People were shouting, horns were honking. Then the wood-sided Jackson family station wagon came into view, turning into the driveway from the road, a long green canoe attached to the roof, green and yellow ribbons flying behind. More cars followed in quick succession.

"Party! Party!" they all shouted, careening up the driveway as we watched helplessly. "Woo-hoo!" Helen yelled from the front seat, waving, honking a portable bicycle horn, as several more cars rounded the driveway into sight, one by one, with bicycle horns honking in each. A festive mob heading straight toward us.

This is now officially an emergency.

· VIII ·

Ceremony

THE MORNING OF the wedding, in the toile guest room at the top of the stairs, my sister Darcy was propped up on one twin bed and my cousin Pierre on the other. Both of them were staring straight ahead, smoking. In my father's sunroom, my half brothers, hunched over coffee mugs, whispered on the phone to the doctor. Someone had started a vacuum cleaner on the long hall down to my mother's bedroom, the familiar whir of the quotidian breaking the quiet of the day. Out the window my nephews sat on surfboards just beyond the break, and my mother walked into the sea.

Down the driveway, the Jackson family was in hiding. They were playing tennis on the court off the patio of the guest cottage, where they had been lodged. They were trying to stay out of the way.

Helen was knitting, her legs stretched long on one of the wicker lounge chairs. Raymond and his youngest son, Chris, were in a heated match against Dean and his best friend, Jim, down from Camden to be the best man. In the tiny kitchenette Dean's oldest brother, also named Raymond but called Raymond Jr. in the family group, was chatting with Josephine, the teenage daughter of the gardener, who had been hired to help out for the wedding. Raymond Jr. and Josephine were working on fixing the juicer. "You know, there are weeks I only drink juice," Raymond Jr. was telling her.

Josephine laughed. "Have you ever heard of food stamps? You're so down to your last dime, you live on juice?"

"No, no," Raymond Jr. was saying, "I do it to cleanse my body."

Josephine rolled her eyes. "That's crazy," she said. "You people out west have some crazy ideas."

Raymond Jr. lived on an island off the coast of Seattle. Ever since he'd left at age fourteen to go to boarding school, he had lived away from home. He had a long beard and piercing blue eyes, giving him a look that was part Paul Newman and part Rasputin. Raymond Jr. rarely came east, most probably to avoid being called Raymond Jr. In the Pacific Northwest, he was studying to be a psychologist with a concentration in family dynamics. He had been hoping for a chance over the wedding weekend to use his own family as guinea pigs. In his backpack upstairs he had brought some cassettes of whale music. He'd read in one of his courses in graduate school that the high frequency of the song of the humpback whale, a sound widely believed to be both complex and beautiful, was known to put people at ease.

The gravel driveway led gently down the hill from the big house and curved slightly to the right to get to the guest cottage, past honeysuckle bushes that grew wild alongside the manicured hedges.

Everyone had trimmed hedges on Lily Pond Lane; it seemed very little was permitted to grow wild for long. Not even the children. Every year at summer's end, before the start of school, all the boys were marched to the barbershop on Newtown Lane and their long sun-bleached curls sheared off to a bowl or buzz cut. The long ponytails we girls wore all summer were loosened from colorful hair fasteners, detangled, and trimmed to shoulder length.

There was a studied sameness to the landscape. Pastel hydrangeas were planted in lines, their stately blossoms waving in the wind off the sea. Mums and marigolds bordered driveways in a trim line under the hedge.

As children, we sought out the wild. The tangles of honeysuckle grew untended and unarranged. We plucked the flowers and sucked the slight drop of sweetness at the stem. We picked the small raspberries that grew in thorny thickets along the bike path to town and the stray potatoes that lay scattered in rows of dust after the farmers had driven their gleaning trucks through the fields at summer's end.

In the mornings, the high two-toned trill of the morning bobwhites announced the day. We rode in bicycle herds of children down the shaded lanes, past the dull thwacks of tennis balls on courts hidden behind topiary, past delivery vans from Dreesen's market turning into long narrow drives. We rode all the way down to the end of Lily Pond Lane, just past Georgica Beach, where to the left it turned onto West End Road. There on the corner was the house of the infamous Cat Lady, as she was called and feared by an entire generation of children. The

Cat Lady's house was a brown shingle saltbox, much like others
in the neighborhood, but whereas the others had neat lines of
hedges, and gravel driveways raked flat and trimmed in white
stones, the vegetation at the Cat Lady's house had grown untended and heavy over the eaves of the house, bowing her roof-
line. The tree branches were gnarled, the grass rough brown
scrub; only the rose hip bushes seemed to show any signs of
life, the small red fruit spotted along the bramble. Despite being forbidden to do so, we would all gather there, daring each
other to go up and knock on her door. We saw cobwebs in the
windows, or so we imagined. Sometimes, we saw stray cats in
the brush, a mother cat with kittens or large toms. Wary and
quiet, the cats hid in the shadows or darted rapidly across the
lawn. "Shhhhhh!" we'd all admonish, because whenever the
cats ran, one or more of the smaller children inevitably called
out or gasped. One boy named Dennis Montgomery claimed
the strange mother and daughter who lived in the dilapidated
house had seen him hiding in the bushes one day and asked him
in for tea. "They have eight million cats," he told us, his eyes
wide. "And garbage everywhere. I mean, everywhere." No one
believed that.

The Montgomerys lived across the street from the Cat Lady's
house, and Barbara Montgomery was a friend of my mother's.
"Mrs. Montgomery says that Dennis has an overactive imagination," our mother would tell us. "I told Mrs. Montgomery,
'Barbara, my three girls are very impressionable,' because you
are, you three girls. You believe anything you hear, especially
if it's a boy who tells you. So I told that Barbara Montgomery, 'Barbara, your boy is telling my three girls some fibs and
I don't care for it at all.' You're not to go there, and it should be

none of your concern what Dennis has to say. Just stay away, as the adults tell you, and whatever Dennis makes up won't alarm you so much." But our alarm was the point. We would wait behind the bramble, holding our bikes at the ready for a getaway, until one or another kid would say, "Look, a curtain moved," or "There goes a cat," and we'd jump on the bikes and squeal them along the curve at the start of Lily Pond Lane, racing each other past the public beach parking lot, past the small lily pond and the potato field, pedaling fast until we were breathless and back at the road of manicured hedges where Lily Pond Lane stretched out parallel to the ocean and life yawned familiar, predictable, and dull.

Years later, the Cat Lady's house became the cultural phenomenon known as Grey Gardens, and the mother and daughter who resided there, the Beales, gained national attention. It ended up Dennis Montgomery had not been lying through his buckteeth about what he'd seen that summer day long ago, when the Beale ladies, Big and Little Edie, as they became known, invited their curious little neighbor in for tea.

Since their arrival, the Jackson family had been playing tennis to pass the time, and wandering the wallpapered rooms of the guest cottage, figuring out what to do next.

Helen hadn't slept well after the rehearsal dinner. The bedrooms in the cottage had wallpaper that covered not just the walls but also the ceiling. The black orchids on the wallpaper in the room she and Raymond were staying in, wallpaper that extended up across the ceiling, looked like fiendish spiders to her by three in the morning. She went down to the kitchenette to make some tea. There she ran into her son Raymond Jr., who was sitting at the small table drinking a beer. She told him about the orchids turning into spiders.

He laughed. "Imagine if you were tripping, Mom," he said. "Those spiders would swoop down and freak the shit out of you."

Helen could not have been more discombobulated by this thought.

Yet by morning she had already moved past her sleepless night, and was overseeing her family playing tennis. For almost thirty years she had been making sure her kids played nicely together, played fair, and she wasn't going to stop simply because they were suddenly adults. "Wait a minute, let's just review the rules here, folks," she was saying. "Dean and Jim are going to cream you two sacks," she said to Raymond and Chris.

"Thank you, Mom, thanks for the encouragement," Chris said.

"You should change sides. Dean-o, play with your father. Even it up."

Whenever Helen wanted to slow the action, she demanded the family stop and review the rules. Over the years most everything got reviewed, rules for games, rules for dinner, rules for life.

"Nice try," Dean said. He lobbed the ball back over the net to his father, who was serving. Raymond Sr.'s baggy shorts and high-top sneakers gave him the air of a prematurely gray toddler. He bounced the ball, then arched his body back, threw the ball above his head, and hit it across the net.

"That's an ace," said Chris. "The old man's still got some steel left in him."

"I ain't dead yet, kids," Raymond said.

"Raymond Jackson," said Helen from her lounge chair, the knitting needles flying, "we're dealing with a family in crisis up that hill. You don't make jokes like that today, honey. Not here. Not now."

Their night, the rehearsal dinner the night before, had been a disappointment for Helen. An unseasonable wind had whipped up on Friday afternoon, making the planned clambake on the beach impossible. The meal was brought in preprepared, from the Seafood Shop on the Montauk Highway, in trays covered in aluminum foil. Three of the round tables under the tent were pressed into use and set for the group of thirty, and the plastic sides of the party tent unfurled so they encased the group, sealed in tight against the elements. The wind off the sea side of the house occasionally buffeted the plastic tarp.

My siblings and I were late returning from the hospital. Dean, his family, and the close friends invited for the evening were already under the tent with my mother and my aunt Jeanne, along with the three blonde wives of my half brothers and the Florida cousins. Everyone wore heavy sweaters and disposable plastic lobster bibs. My mother glared at us as we walked into the tent, fresh from the ICU, and took me aside before I could join the group. "It's about damn time," she said. "What were you kids thinking, leaving me here with these people? You had all afternoon with your father while Sissy and I have had to hold down the fort and entertain. Is it my wedding?"

"Actually, you told me last week it was."

"No guff. You know what I mean. Is all of this"—she flitted her hand toward the table across the tent, where Dean's family sat—"*my* responsibility? No. It's yours."

Across the tent, Dean and his family sat with a few of my

cousins, all in sweaters and bibs. I felt if I could just get there, get over to that side of the tent, I would be safe. I could cut a line straight through her anger to the other side.

When she saw me walking across to her, Helen's mouth opened in a wide smile. "Oh, goodie," she said to everyone, "here she comes, folks, here comes our bride!" She put her arm around me. "Someone get the bride a bib and a drink," she said to the table. "We want our city girl to feel special tonight." Helen could put the world back in some kind of predictable order, I thought. I could join this family of homemade sweaters and pie recipes and special clambakes by the sea.

Watching my father in the hospital that afternoon, we were unable to leave. His hair was dry, matted down, his mouth slack, his shoulders heaving, his head hanging off to one side at an awkward angle. There was a slow stench of stale, which I imagine I knew even then was death slipping into the antiseptic room and tinging the air. Once the sight of him became something we had gotten used to, the smell reigned in that quiet room. At some point much later it occurred to me I should have looked for the yellow legal pad back in his room. He had said he was working on the toast for the rehearsal dinner the last time I'd spoken to him, and knowing him, it would be there somewhere among the books and index cards and vials of prescription pills. But we lingered, transfixed and awkward in the hospital room, and there was no time to rummage up in his room, if I had even had the heart.

Under the tent that night my siblings and I gamely tied the plastic Seafood Shop bibs around our necks, and in some fashion the hospital visit receded temporarily even as it still glazed the air, a glow just past that of the votive candles illuminating the tent's festivities. Like my father himself, the memory of him in his hospital bed was present that night but not, palpable yet visible only to those with the eyes to see. Soon the lobsters were passed and the bright shells cracked, the wine was poured, and the toasts started. Laughter began. Under the tent the evening warmed. Occasionally the wind off the beach buffeted the flaps of the tent, blowing an eerie chill through the flushed crowd.

I woke up the morning of my wedding and I realized I had lost my voice. It was a sparkling clear day out as I stood at the window and watched the beach for a while.

The waves were gentle. My nephews were already up and paddling their surfboards out past the first break. I watched my mother walk down to the beach and stand at the water's edge, tucking her hair under her bathing cap. Downstairs in the kitchen, I heard the screen door open and bang shut a few times as it always did on busy mornings. A teakettle whistled. "Get out of my kitchen!" I heard Johanna say. And I heard Laura, the housekeeper, reprimand her, "Hey, woman, be nice to him, he's just a boy!" We all had a long day ahead.

"You sound fine to me," said Nat Thorpe, the new minister at the Episcopal church in town. He had a beard and thick sandy hair that fell in a hank over his forehead. He constantly pushed it back as he spoke.

I went to visit him in the late morning, to tell him I had lost my voice.

"I mean," I said, "I can't hear myself. I can't hear myself think. I need to talk this out."

He smiled. "Okay," he said.

"I don't even know you. But here I am."

"Let's see what we can do," he said. "About your voice. Getting it back. First, how's everyone at home?" He nodded. "This is a big day."

I sat in the blondewood-paneled office, the beveled Tiffany glass windows looking out across a small field to the town windmill.

Though I didn't know Nat—we weren't a religious family—he had agreed to conduct the wedding ceremony.

"Tell me about your father," he said. "I've not yet had the pleasure of meeting the man." Nat used the word "yet" and I focused on that. Nat thought he was going to come out of this, maybe. Or maybe he was just saying that for my benefit. "What did he teach you?" Nat asked.

What did my father teach me? "He taught me, don't expect too much."

We had been in the sunroom when my father first told me this. I was just twenty, too old for some things, too young for others. Same as any age.

He had handed me the most recent installment of Franklin the octopus that day. I pleaded for the stories long past the age when I would by any count want to hear a children's story, but I kept at it to coax his imagination out, as if Franklin could somehow keep him going, even as I saw him recede. His handwriting, on the envelope, was shaky, the letters already like skeletons. "I finally managed this last installment," he had written on the envelope. "With love and pride, Daddy."

"Don't expect too much," he said as I took the envelope, "because you'll just be disappointed." And he bowed his head.

It was then, that moment, that I saw his life was not about

expectation anymore; it was about disappointment. Yet Franklin defied that. In the stories, even the last one, his voice was clear. The charming, charismatic voice that was my father's. Deep inside a well, covered up by alcohol, somewhere in there, his imagination still existed whole, and I saw it struggling to come out. That was the point of Franklin, anyway, of asking him to write the stories. To focus his mind, to coax out a few more marvels. I knew that when I asked him to write the stories. Franklin was how I'd keep him close, long after he was no longer there.

"My father taught me not to expect much," I told Nat, the minister. "And I don't."

"That's good," the minister said. "That's good advice. Your father sounds like a very wise man."

"He's in a coma," I reminded the minister. "He's in a coma, and yesterday my brother made us buy chicken."

"Chicken?"

"In case we got hungry. As if we were going to be passing around greasy legs and thighs while my father lay attached to a machine, struggling to breathe."

Watching a person in a coma, I realized then, plays tricks. No matter the machines, the cords and nozzles, a person in a coma looks like he is sleeping. It is impossible not to stare and try to will him awake.

Maybe that's what Scott was thinking. Let's just make a picnic of it, and maybe he'll wake up and join in. Of course he knew better, but everyone grasps for their own way to deflect the weight of such a situation.

"And you're getting married today." It wasn't a question but a statement.

"Apparently. Yeah. I'm supposed to be getting married to-day," I told the minister. "It's like this wave is coming, and I can't stop it."

Nat waited. He folded his hands in his lap and assumed a psychiatric silence. Finally he said, "Are you here to ask my permission or my advice?"

I laughed. "Give me whatever you've got. I'm here because I got nothing."

"You're laughing," he said. "You're laughing, but I know you don't think this is funny."

"I'm supposed to get married today," I repeated. "Everyone is here, the in-laws, the relatives, the tent is on the lawn, and boom."

"Boom?"

"Yeah, boom. It's all happening and I can't stop it. Boom. That's all I got."

"Okay, let's back it up. Do you want to stop it?"

Did I want to stop it? No one had asked me that.

"That's why you think you've lost your voice. Because no one is asking to hear it. But I want to hear it. What do you want to do?"

I sighed. "This is why I'm here. I don't know."

"Why do you want to marry Dean," he asked, "do you think?"

I had an answer for that, though I did not know it until it came out of my mouth.

"I am in the sea," I said. "Just like the sea by the house, the sea I've looked at my whole life from my childhood bedroom. But I'm in the sea, not looking from the house. A tidal wave is coming, it will pull me under, and I will drown. Dean comes by in a motorboat. He throws me a rope and starts the engine, and up I go. Far, far offshore, away from the long gray house, away from the tidal wave, skimming along the top of the water, racing away."

We live on such a perilous dune.

Nat sat listening, his hands still clasped in his lap.

"Okay," he said after a while. "I'm going to say something that's obvious, though I suspect right now it may not seem that way to you. Listen, whether or not you marry Dean today, or ever, is not going to change your father's prognosis. He's on his own path now. It's my opinion that you should stay on yours."

"I should water-ski, in other words."

He smiled. "Yeah," he said. "Water-ski. I like that. Water-ski." Then he laughed. "Not boom, but zoom!" He loved his own joke. "Zoom!" he repeated a few more times. "I've got to remember that."

As I was leaving, he called after me. "Hey," he said, "you know, it's possible to get out into deep water and not drown."

At precisely 4 p.m. that afternoon, my mother fit the wedding veil on my head. I was looking in the mirror in her bathroom as she did this. All I could see behind me were her hands pulling on my hair, poking pins in my head. Her earrings, big gold hoops, dangled in and out of sight as she moved around behind me.

"You should have let me get a proper hairdresser in here, dearie," she said. "It's far too late now. Jesus." And she withdrew to her bedroom.

On the small table near her shantung chaise, there was a silver tray and small cut-crystal glasses. My aunt Jeanne sat on the chaise, an emerald green bottle of brandy in her hand. Only a few remnants of the label of the bottle remained, browned with age, the words faded to illegibility. This brandy had belonged to their father, Simon Pierre Robineau. My aunt Jeanne had carried it on the plane from Miami in her lap. It was all they had left of their father, the Frenchman who raised them under the leafy canopy of banyan trees in Coconut Grove: a bottle of old brandy. In Robineau family tradition, the brandy was poured out for a toast whenever a girl in the family wed. It was a ritual to be done just before the wedding ceremony, in private. Only Robineau women, the groom, and his female relatives were allowed to take part.

We gathered in her pink room—me, my sisters, Dean's sister Jessica, my mother, and my aunt Jeanne. Nonnie and Helen were ushered in from the guest house. They formed a small semicircle around me. I was seated on the chaise. "Dean must not see the dress," my mother said. She draped a sheet over my shoulders.

"Wait, are you sure this is the way the tradition is supposed to go?" my sister Catherine asked. "It seems to me the rule is that the bride and groom should not see each other before the wedding. It has nothing to do with not seeing each other's wedding clothes."

"Catherine, dearie," my mother said, "for pity's sake, of course it is supposed to go like this. It's family tradition. The groom does not see the dress. Don't try to stir things up. We know, because we are *la famille Robineau* and we made the tradition up. Right, Sissy?"

"Right-o," said my aunt Jeanne, who always agreed with everything my mother had to say.

Dean came in. He was in a black morning coat, with gray pinstripe pants. He looked shy in the room of women. He looked at me wrapped in a sheet and winked. He knew to say nothing that would set my mother on edge.

"Look at you," said his grandmother Nonnie as he walked up beside her. She clicked her tongue. "My, but don't you look like the prince of England." She blinked at him through her thick glasses.

The brandy was poured around. It glowed in the cut crystal, the warm color of caramel. We drank a toast to Colonel Robineau, may he rest in peace.

"Wow," said my sister Darcy. "This shit tastes like a linen closet."

I sat on the chaise, the ungainly bedsheet drooping over my delicate lace dress. "What the hell does a linen closet taste like?" I asked my sister.

"You know. Old. Musty." She took another sip and added, "Gross."

"It happens to be very fine brandy," my mother said. "It's Napoleon brandy from 1872. It does not taste like a linen closet."

"Well," said my aunt, "that does happen to be where I store it."

"Oh god, Sissy, not anymore. Jesus," my mother said. "One of you two girls"—she looked at my sisters—"you're up next. In fact, I think we should just keep the brandy here in my cabinet while we wait for the next round. One of them is bound to find a nice boy soon. Pray to god."

Downstairs the string quartet began tuning up in the garden.

Soon there was the mumble and chat of guests being seated in rows of white wooden folding chairs that gave out to the sea. The waves were breaking in a calm, easy rhythm, the lulling cadence we fell asleep to as children.

The string quartet was made up of Juilliard students who had come out from New York for the day. Earlier they had stowed their black instrument cases and their duffle bags of formal clothes in a room down the hall at the other side of the house, the "servants' wing," as it was called, and taken towels to swim. I watched them as they ran into the sea, all knees and elbows, their bodies gangly and pale, untouched by the summer sun.

Soon after, the bagpiper arrived and joined them on the beach. He was a heavyset man with a graying rust-colored mustache. He wore a T-shirt tight over his midsection, ample tufts of chest hair curling out at the top.

Ruth Ann Middleton bustled into my mother's bedroom in a bright orange muumuu and white kid gloves, a white pocketbook dangling from her forearm, a pad of paper in her hand, the top pages flung over and bobbing as she patrolled the proceedings. She repeated her credo that weddings always start on time, and looked people up and down as she shuffled in and out, herding "the nonessentials," as she called those not in the wedding party, out of the bedroom and downstairs.

Dean, in Ruth Ann's opinion, was a nonessential, and she glowered at him while he lingered in the pink room. I took his hand once and squeezed it before he left. He looked at me, his eyes looking right into mine. "See you downstairs," he whispered in my ear, his lips brushing the veil.

Helen moved her mother along, holding her arm gently as

they eased out of the pink room. "C'mon, Mother," she said, gently pushing her mother from behind. Nonnie was dressed in a canary yellow dress and a white sweater she had crocheted years ago for special occasions such as weddings. Her mouth turned up slightly at the edges in a half smile. It gave her a spritely, mischievous air. She moved tentatively at her daughter's prods.

"Don't you think you should change?" Ruth Ann asked my cousin Pierre, who had showed up in an orange-and-white-striped jacket and no tie. "Because there's not much time, and weddings start on time. You should get on your wedding clothes," she said. "Whoever you are."

"I am dressed," he said. "I'm a cousin."

"He's mine," Aunt Jeanne said. "My eldest boy." Aunt Jeanne and Uncle Jooge had five children. Pierre was my favorite, my dearest relative, more like a brother than a cousin. It was he who showed up for all the "brother" things, like birthdays and graduations. He had recently moved to San Francisco, where he was slowly and somewhat noisily emerging from the closet.

"There are no exceptions to this," Ruth Ann warned. "Weddings begin as planned." At the window, my sisters stood in bare feet, in their matching pink bridesmaid dresses, watching people being seated below.

"There's Lou Anne," Catherine said.

"Where?" asked our mother. "Is that girl wearing one of her hats I hope not?"

My mother's friend Lou Anne Wall had a green Astroturf lawn in her living room and a yellow piano, and tended to wear loud hats with feathers and tiny papier-mâché animals in the brim.

"She's wearing one that looks like a satellite dish," Catherine answered.

"Oh god, let me get a look," our mother said, and pushed the curtain aside. "Jesus Christ, that girl always has to steal the show. And look, there's your aunt Sally, girls, in a mink coat. What is she trying to prove, a mink in August. That is so tacky. So vintage Sally, really, if you want to hear what I really think. That girl is the limit."

Aunt Sally, my father's younger sister, was one of my mother's nemeses. She had her bleached-blonde hair in a bouffant coif. Despite the fierce look always on her face, she in fact resembled my father. Their features were similar. "Daddy in pearls," we called her. Every year she and my mother bought each other an ounce of caviar from the 21 Club for Christmas, and waited to see who could hold out the longest before writing a thank-you note.

"There's a British word for those wedding hats. Astonishers or something," my sister Darcy said.

"They are called fascinators," chimed in Ruth Ann Middleton, "and really, no one should be wearing a hat to a wedding at this hour. It's an evening wedding. And it will be a night wedding if people don't listen."

Ruth Ann appeared to be getting agitated.

"Pat!" she said to my mother. "So much planning goes into these things. Please, we're in the final stretch now."

I wondered if Ruth Ann was even aware of where my father was. I assumed she had to be in on it, as it involved a major change in the roster of the wedding party. I wondered if that was adding to her being flustered, or if she was always frantic at the beginning of one of her weddings. If, like an actor who ran his lines backstage before he went on, or a singer who runs through the scales, or an athlete who stretches on the sidelines of the playing field before the big game, Ruth Ann was doing a warm-up routine on my mother's pink rug.

"Okay, kids," my mother said to us. "Please listen to Ruth Ann. She's worked very hard on this, we owe it to her." Ruth Ann stood beside my mother with her lists and her pocketbook. "It's her show."

It was Ruth Ann's show. We owed it to her.

"Wait, excuse me, it's Ruth Ann's what?" said my sister Darcy. Darcy could always be counted on to speak her mind.

"Quiet," my mother said.

Darcy looked at me. "You know?" she said. She was still in her bare feet, her satin bridesmaid shoes lying on their sides under the chaise longue. "What the fuck does that mean, Ruth Ann's show? It's *your* wedding, for chrissake."

"Jesus," my mother said. "Enough." She turned to Ruth Ann. "I'm sorry," she said. "These kids are a little unnerved."

"Oh," Ruth Ann said, "Pat, dear, please don't worry. It's quite normal for there to be nerves at a wedding." She gave a merry laugh, as if everything were proceeding perfectly, just as planned, just a few jitters, everything was normal for a wedding.

A little after 4:30 Ruth Ann ushered my sisters from my mother's bedroom. Weddings always start on time or her name wasn't Ruth Ann Middleton, Ruth Ann emphasized one more time to the room, to my sisters and our mother and me. Ruth Ann used her girth as a guard against debate as she led them out of the room, her notepad still clutched in her gloved hand.

Somewhere down below, Dean was standing strong against

the summer sky in a gray morning suit. Only my mother and I remained upstairs in her bedroom.

I had sand in my hair. In her bathroom mirror, I fussed with it.

Over the years, we had glued our found seashells around the frame of the mirror above the sink in my mother's bathroom, and I studied them as I brushed. Luminescent shards of slipper shells pink like baby fingernails, rosy whelks, dusty white clamshells, gray scallop shells that spread like fans. The offerings of childhood.

In the bedroom, my mother dialed her pink princess phone. I could hear the click of the clear Lucite dial, yellowed with age.

The quartet started in on the opening piece on the list. Soft and stately, the light melody lilting a graceful sorrow over the rows of guests assembling on white folding chairs on the grass.

"This is Mrs. McCulloch," I heard my mother say into her princess phone. "I'm trying to reach Dr. Albert in the ICU." After a moment she spoke again. "So kindly get him. *Now*," she said. My mother spoke in the clipped British accent she used to sound imperious.

Evidently, we were going to get through this with grace and style, even if it meant pulling out the clipped British accent.

"I wish to speak to him urgently," she said. "It's of utmost importance he get this."

She waited. The violin and the cello and the sea were the only sounds as I brushed my hair, there was the occasional whisper and cough from the guests below. *They're here*, I thought as I brushed. *Zoom*.

"What? No, he can't call me back. I will not be available in an hour. Find him. Jesus Christ! I need to speak to him now. No, I'll not leave a message.

"Dearie," she called in to me. "Leave that hair alone. I put that veil in place very carefully. It's too late now to fix the hair. It's a lost cause and you're just making it worse. Next time, listen to me in the first place. I am trying to cover a lot of bases here and your hair is no longer up on my priority list."

When the attending physician came on the phone, my mother asked him, "Are you on call all night?"

He must have reassured her that he'd call if there was any change in my father's condition because she said, "No, that's just the point." She listened a bit more and then said, "Doctor, that is not the point of my call. Why don't you stop talking and listen to me? If anything happens to my husband this evening, do not call this house. Do not. Do you hear me? We cannot be disturbed."

The quartet finished their song and launched into another. She was quiet on the phone for a while and then she repeated, "It's immaterial and I'm sorry, Doctor. We cannot be disturbed, though. We are having a party." And she hung up the phone.

"What's immaterial?" I yelled from the bathroom. "What are you sorry about?"

"Never mind that," she said. "Keep your mind on what's happening right now. And what's happening is your brother is supposed to be here right now. Damn it."

Soon there was a knock on her bedroom door. My half brother Keith. As if to explain his appearance he said to my mother, "That woman down there—"

"Ruth Ann," my mother corrected. "She's not 'that woman.'"

"Ruth Ann then. Whoever she is, she says weddings start on time."

"She is a professional," my mother said. "I hope to dear god you were polite."

Keith laughed. He had a light, high laugh, the laugh of our father. The laughter we used to hear as children, falling asleep to the sounds of tinkling glasses and plates in the dining room below as we lay together in quilts. Keith inherited both our father's laugh and our father's pale blue eyes. "She's pacing in the living room yelling at everyone," he said. "She practically lifted me by the lapels and carried me up here."

"Because she's a professional and she's trying her best with what we've given her, poor thing. All right, now that you're here, I'm going down. Go get your sister out of the bathroom. It's her wedding, for pity's sake. Everyone's knocked themselves out. It would be nice if she managed to show up."

She went down the stairs in her "no-color blue" dress to be seated in the front row beside the housekeeper, the gardener, and the rest of her kitchen staff. It was part of my mother's vision, her Lady Bountiful message, long thought out, I imagine, and acted on for all her friends to see, that she would array her domestic staff up front by her side. The rest of the family sat a row behind.

Keith came to the door of the bathroom. My hair was just not going to get in line with the program. Beach hair, springing back against the brush with a mind of its own. The light veil hovered on my head like a tea napkin. My brother Keith was trim in his morning suit; his short brown beard was cut close to his face and flecked with blond.

The quartet was playing the song I had chosen for my sisters to walk up the aisle to. I could see them in my mind's eye, stepping up to the rose-entwined gazebo, the pink ribbons flapping in the slight wind off the sea.

At the door to the bathroom, my brother Keith watched me watch myself in the mirror.

"Crazy hair," I said to Keith. I tossed the brush in the sink. My mother's bathroom sink was also pink. "Hopeless."

Below, the music then stopped. Nat, the minister, cleared his throat; then he spoke to the crowd. "On behalf of the family, I'd like to welcome you here this afternoon. John McCulloch is our captain, the paterfamilias of the McCulloch family. He cannot be here with us today," he said, "yet it is his wish, and the wish of his family, that we join together to celebrate this very special occasion."

In the crowd, there were murmurs.

"We better get going," Keith said to me quietly.

The music started up again. The quartet played the opening of Bach's Double Violin Concerto in D Minor. It was our cue.

I had chosen the second movement of Bach's Double Violin Concerto to march in to because it was slow. I hadn't wanted my father to stumble walking down the aisle. I had assumed he'd be drunk by this time of day, 5 p.m., and I would have to marshal all my strength to hold him steady as we walked, everyone's eyes on us. I had imagined this months before when I had thought of this moment. Maybe years, in fact.

They say it's a moment a little girl imagines all the years she is growing up. A moment a woman remembers forever.

Keith eyed me; both of us had the glazed looks of zombies. "Are you ready, kiddo?" he asked at the door of the bathroom. He held out his arm.

We walked down the long hall past my father's empty room, down the stairs and out the side door while the quartet riffed on Bach's concerto, waiting for us. They struck up the second movement as soon as we came into sight at the door of the patio. The sun was doing what it was supposed to, casting a golden light across the lawn.

And because weddings start on time, this one did.

· IX ·

The Day After

THE SUN SHOT a bright streak across the antique wallpaper. We were in an unfamiliar bedroom in the American Hotel in Sag Harbor, a fifteen-minute drive from the house. An un-opened bottle of Champagne, compliments of the manage-ment, sat in a bath of melted ice in a silver bucket. Beside it, two flutes. We had come in late, driving in my old maroon Saab, and now dried shaving cream crusted on the rearview window in the gravel parking lot below. People had thrown rose petals, a Ruth Ann Middleton touch, and they stuck on the windshield in splotches. On a brocade armchair in the far corner of the room, my wedding dress lazed, sandy at the hem and delicately collapsed like a worn-out party girl.

As the sky lightened on the first day of our marriage, I was thinking about death.

I need to go back over to the house, I was thinking. My family would just be waking; the party rental pickup staff would be collecting the used table linens and rolling the tables back into the van. In the hospital, nurses would be silently moving in and out of my father's room. The heart monitor would be steadily beeping. I wanted to know if any of our family was there: Did anyone get up and go see him? Did anyone call to make sure he was all right?

If anything happens to my husband this evening, do not call this house. We are having a party.

I sat cross-legged on the bed. I twisted a strand of hair with my finger, a childhood habit, as the sun rose higher and the bright streak grew longer across the room. Beside me, Dean slept. *He sleeps like a child sometimes*, I was thinking. The deep crease between his eyes smoothed out only in sleep.

The plan, now canceled, had been to go from the American Hotel directly to the LIE and from there to the airport and from there to our honeymoon. We had a borrowed villa in Santa Margherita Ligure, south of Rapallo, lent by a friend of my parents for a ten-day stay. That we needed to get back to the house instead struck me as both unfair and urgent.

The night before, when Dean and I had left the reception, we'd driven down a side road to the beach. The tide was out, and the moon illuminated my white dress as we walked to the water's edge. He rolled his trousers; I held my hem up to midthigh, the scalloped edges draped over my forearms as we waded in to our knees. The sounds of the party were distant, and down the beach the lights from the neighboring houses were all going out. Bedtime. We watched the water for a long time before we got back in the car and drove to the hotel. I wished, at that moment, that I were one of the guests on the dance floor, not the one for whom the day, the week, held such a complexity of import. I thought of the girls whose stories I had heard, those whose wedding dresses had fallen off while they danced. Under the tent, they were playing a loud reggae beat; there was whooping and laughter. I thought, *So much planning, and I don't remember a single thing. The wedding is over. How was it, I don't remember—did I have any fun?*

I stared at Dean's sleeping form, willing him awake. And so Dean woke up the first morning of our marriage with his wife staring at him.

He reached out as he came awake and lightly held my ankle. I could tell by this small gesture that he remembered too, immediately upon waking, what we were up against. We both looked down and saw our wedding bands at the same time. I put my hand close to his. Two bright gold rings, entirely new, unscathed.

"Mine looks so little," I said.

"Mine feels huge," Dean said. He took his hand away and swiveled the ring on his finger. "It feels like a cigar band," he said. He flexed and unflexed his fingers. Then he darted his hands up in the air. "Weird."

"Does it bug you?"

"No, I'm just thinking, it might mess with my jump shot is all."

His hands made shadows along the wallpaper as he poked the air. The ring shone in the sunlight.

"I've just never worn a ring before. I'll get used to it."

· · ·

"We're down here," Helen said into the phone, "hiding out in the guest quarters, honey. Daddy's playing tennis with the kids."

On the tennis court, the Jacksons were once again playing doubles. When we arrived, Helen had resumed her position on the slatted lounge chair, knitting. It seemed to be her safe place for the weekend. Upstairs in the big house, it seemed possible that my mother had forgotten that any of them existed.

On the tennis court, Raymond hit one past his son and Helen called it out from the sidelines.

"C'mon, Mom, cut the guy some slack," Chris said.

"Cut me some slack, Mother," Raymond said. "I'm on vacation."

Helen's sister-in-law, Dean's aunt Anita, was hollering at her husband outside as they packed up their car.

Helen ran out to the gravel road, the pleats of her tennis skirt flapping against her leg. "QUIET," she said. She held her hands to her cheeks. "There's a family in crisis up the hill, Neet. Please."

The night before, as Dean and I were preparing to drive away, outside the car, through the windshield, Helen was waving. "See you on the flip-flop," she kept shouting, "go have fun!" as the wedding guests swirled around her with fistfuls of rose petals they threw at the car.

Now, the day after, she stood in the driveway outside the cottage, watching as her brother and sister-in-law loaded her mother, Nonnie, into the car and drove away, back to Rhode Island. She waited a while as their car rumbled down the driveway, then watched it turn onto Lily Pond Lane. She came back to the tennis court.

"Time-out. Let's just review the rules," she said. She clasped her hands.

Raymond and her kids paused their game and stood quietly while she walked out onto the court. "I want to get out of here," she said to her husband. To me she said, "Honey, you guys have a lot on your plate. We need to leave."

Up at the house, my mother had written out the day's menu in green Magic Marker on a yellow legal pad, as she did every morning. It included chicken salad and French madeleines with local raspberries for lunch, and stuffed striped bass for dinner followed by sugar pie.

In the kitchen, the yellow sheet was taped on the white Formica kitchen cabinet. Johanna tied her hair in netting for the day, then sat down to cut the crusts off thin slices of white sandwich bread.

On the beach my teenage nephews, usually on their surfboards at this hour, lay ever so slightly hungover on large orange towels, napping in the sun. They lay with their arms slung over their eyes, some curled on their sides like castaways. They wore T-shirts and baggy trunks, a few in baseball caps, the visors pulled low over their foreheads.

"The sign of a good wedding," my cousin Pierre was telling my sister Darcy, "is bonking." The two of them were on lounge chairs on the front deck of the house. As I arrived, he asked me, "Hey, there you are. Did anyone, to your knowledge, bonk last night?"

He circled one bare foot in the air as he spoke. "It should have been me, but it wasn't me," he reported. "God knows I tried. It would have been me if there had been any cute gay boys in the house."

He thought. "I could have had William Gaines."

"Whoa, what about William Gaines?" I said. He was the husband of our second cousin Diane.

Pierre shook his head. "He's gay." He lit a cigarette. The plume of his exhale circled lazily in the breeze.

"No way, sorry," Darcy said. "That's a big fat lie."

"Scout's honor," said Pierre. "I never get my gaydar wrong, girls. The only people who don't know it are his wife and the rest of you all. In fact, let me revise that. I'd actually put money on the fact that Diane knows. She's not in that marriage for bonking purposes, I can promise you. I never get gay wrong. But Raymond Jr. is the hot one."

"He's not gay, I promise you."

"Which is such a total waste. That beard of his. Hot."

A brilliant summer day opened up as the sun rose high. The contrail behind a plane fragmented in the blue sky as it passed far off over the sea.

"Okay, so maybe I did bonk someone," he said.

"Someone?"

"But not William Gaines and not Raymond Jr. So the rest is immaterial. All in all, I just did it to bless the wedding. The proceedings needed a little flesh on flesh in the dunes."

"Thanks for taking care of that for us, sweetheart," I said. "Because I feel pretty certain Ruth Ann Middleton forgot to put that on her to-do list. 'Beach bonking at ten p.m. Bonking starts on time or my name isn't Ruth Ann Middleton.'"

"That woman was a mess of fabric with five o'clock shadow," Pierre said. "Where do they dig up people like that? I was impressed by the horror." Then he added, "Technically, it was closer to midnight."

"What was?"

"The bonking."

"Don't say 'bonk,' dearie." My mother came out on the porch. "It's ved-dy unattractive." She stood with her hands on her hips and looked at me.

"*There* you are, Mrs. Jackson," she said. "It's high time."

"I'm not Mrs. Jackson, Ma, if it's me you're speaking to."

"I daresay it's not I," Pierre added.

"'I daresay it's not *me*,' as in 'It's not me to *whom* she is speaking.' You know that, Pierre. C'mon."

"Whatever," I said. "I'm keeping my name."

"Oh Lord, dearie," she said next. "Don't be so extravagant. I simply don't have the energy for any attitude today." She sat down on the edge of Pierre's chaise and put her hand out for his cigarette. She took a long drag. "There's way too much to do, and for starters you need to get your wedding presents out of the way. They're cluttering up the dining room and the foyer."

"Have you even called about our father?" I asked.

"He's holding steady. I spoke to the ICU doctor on duty." She lowered her voice. "Speaking of which, when are *they* leaving?" She pointed Pierre's cigarette in the direction of the cottage. "I can't have them here past lunch. I simply cannot. There's much too much to do around your father. This is a household in crisis, not a welcome wagon. It's your responsibility to get them out the door."

She looked at Pierre. "Pierre, dearie, you can help move her presents up to the attic, can't you? Except for the canoe. My god. A canoe. Who gives such presents. The canoe needs to go in the garage. I'm sure all those big strapping boys down there in that family can take care of that."

"Ma," I said, "do you think William Gaines is gay?"

She thought about it. Then she scrunched her nose and smiled. "Don't you think?"

"Wait, you do?" Darcy said. She leaned forward. "No shit?"

"I think he and Diane have an 'arrangement,' as we used to say back in my day."

"Wow. Pierre nailed it then."

"Nailed it, not him," Pierre said. "There's a difference, people."

"'Nail.' 'Bonk.' Jesus, you kids," my mother said.

We all looked up at the flawless sky.

"We need to go back over there," my sister Darcy said after a while. "He's all alone."

My half brother Scott wanted to stop again to pick up lunch. An Italian sub from Villa Italia by the East Hampton train station.

"We don't know how long we're going to be there," he said. We were in T-shirts in the sandy family station wagon. I can't remember who was driving, but I remember the mood was not grim, exactly, but unreal. Any element of levity—the summer tunes on the radio, the Sunday morning beach traffic on the highway—seemed an ironic background buzz. On the top-ten station, the Police's "Every Breath You Take" was playing, which seemed to have its own grim irony as we drove along.

Once again, we'd arrive at the ICU with a bag of uneaten food that smelled of summer picnics. I once again pictured the six of us wreathed around my father on his hospital bed in a coma as Scott distributed the cuts of sub, the oil shiny on the paper wrap, the air thick with the smell of genoa salami and roasted red pepper. This time, not even the smell would remind us of anything but the person in front of us.

Every breath you take.

"No stopping," our mother said as we left. "You kids had better make tracks and get back here for luncheon." She ran out into the driveway as we were pulling away. "Do not leave Sissy and me alone with the Jacksons." To me she added, "This is your responsibility, not mine, remember." We left her, hands on hips, under the Portuguese tile that read "Quinta de Cri-anças Brincar." We drove down the driveway past the party tent on the lawn, the flaps billowing gently in the morning air. The rose petals still clung in spots to the gravel as we turned past the driveway sign near the thicket of wild honeysuckle, past the guest cottage, and out onto Lily Pond Lane toward Route 27 to Southampton Hospital.

The last time I saw my father that day, his position had not much changed since the day before, other than they'd propped him up on his pillows a bit. Still his head lobbed to one side, his mouth slack. His lips were chapped. The hospital gown hung loose off his shoulders, and his dried hair was standing up on his head, rubbed that way from the pillow, no doubt, though it reminded me of the hairdos we used to give him when we were young, climbing up behind him on the couch, our backs resting against the bookshelf as we combed his hair. Now it seemed strangely yellowed, stale somehow.

I rubbed my father's shoulder. I had stared at Dean that very morning to try to will him awake, so perhaps somewhere inside

I hoped I could come to the hospital, stare at my father, and miraculously will him awake. Hope. It all seemed absolutely potentially reversible if I stared at him hard enough, and yet at the same time it was so obviously irreversible. The smell of the Italian subs, the ticking of the monitor, the occasional shuffle of nurses in and out, the group of us staring at our father. That was all.

Every breath you take.

Earlier that day, my mother had driven over to see my father, but had not told us at the time. I heard about her visit years later, from one of her friends. I had always wondered when she had said good-bye to him, when between the wedding details and the follow-up she had seen him.

Later that day, long after my siblings and I had returned from the hospital to the house, Dean had driven over to see him but had not told me until later either.

None of us were with him when, still later, he died.

My mother, visiting in the very early morning, had yelled. Evidently she had the impression, as many do, that if you yell loudly at a coma victim, you have a better chance of being heard.

Dean, when he visited, had matched my father's labored breathing. In his studies in neurolinguistics, he had learned that if you match the breathing of someone in a coma, you have a better chance of being heard.

My mother yelled about remembering things. She yelled that she hoped he remembered how many times they had promised each other, if either was to be incapacitated beyond recovery, the other would sign the "Do Not Resuscitate" document that guaranteed no extreme measure would be taken.

Dean heaved as my father heaved, while behind him the nurses shuffled out and left him alone. All he had said at first to my father's heaving body was, "Just stay in the moment."

But what was "the moment," exactly? The Jacksons had packed up, having hauled the green canoe, supposed to be the centerpiece of the festivities, off the top of the car. Vincent, the gardener, had helped them haul it into the garage, the ribbons still on. No one had bothered to untie them. There the canoe would stay out of sight as the scene changed from a wedding, a boat to paddle into the happy beginning of a new life, over to something that was, if not death, then something very close to the end of life.

Dean had taken long, steady breaths as he spoke to my father, matching his breathing, breath for breath, speaking in a calm, even voice. As his family was heading back across the Long Island Sound on the ferry to New England, and Pierre and I were stowing the wedding presents in the attic, and my mother was speaking on the pink princess phone in her bedroom to the lawyer—who guaranteed her he would be returning early from vacation on Cape Cod first thing in the morning to help her get things sorted out—Dean sat with my father in the hospital. He told him the score of the Yankees game. They were both fans, and he passed news to my father, often sending him postcards with the score on it when my father was traveling during baseball season. In July, when my father had been at the Carlton House and too drunk to leave his apartment, Dean would go over and watch the game with him, seated on the couch while my father nodded in and out of sleep, his jaw resting on the lapel of his smoking jacket, eyes cloudy and half open.

"Well, it's done, John, I got the kids married," my mother yelled.

"I'd like to tell you about the wedding, John, you would have been proud," Dean said.

"Remember? You didn't want us to do anything heroic to save you if you no longer had your dignity," my mother yelled. "Just like I didn't if it was me."

Dean said, his breath heaving, "The day was bright, the weather held, and the sun set just as we said our vows."

"Remember, that was the promise we made to each other. No extreme measures. We promised to let each other go if it was past all hope of a good life," she yelled.

I wonder if, outside my father's room, the nurses clotted together at the doorway listening to this last exchange between a husband and wife: "So we're not going to do that, John. Tonight, we're going to unhook all these things and let you go."

"So, it's okay, you can go now," Dean said softly to my father. "It was a beautiful wedding and we could feel you there. Everyone thought about you, and it really, really is okay to go now. We love you, John."

"Remember that we love you, John," my mother said.

"Remember that we love you, John," Dean said.

"The kids are coming over, but after that, the hospital team is taking you off all these machines," my mother told my father.

"We all wish you'd been there at the wedding, John," Dean said.

"I couldn't believe you weren't there with me at our daughter's wedding, John," my mother said.

"Just before the wedding started, the minister talked about you, how you couldn't be with us, but it was your wish, and that of your family, that the wedding go on," Dean told him. "We figured you'd want us to go ahead. So, you were there with us too, in spirit."

"The doctors have given up hope!" my mother yelled.

"I have such great hopes for you," he had told me the last time we'd spoken, the week before the wedding, "and great hopes for your life."

"I hope you know how much we love you," is the last thing I had told my father, when I could think of nothing else to say.

"We love you very much, John," my mother said.

"We love you very much, John," Dean said.

I would like to know what else my mother said that day. I hope that she told him she loved him, and squeezed his hand and called him *Jean-Jean*, as she did when she was being affectionate. But I don't know. I do know she signed the DNR order and returned home, to where the rose petals from the end of the party were still sticking on the gravel of the driveway, flattened by the tire treads of so many cars leaving late at night, long after the petals had been thrown at Dean and me, pelted in our wake as we ran toward our car.

That night, long after the Jacksons had departed, we had a quiet dinner in the house by the sea. My half siblings, my mother, my sisters, Dean, and me. It was very quiet that night. After dinner, we sat in the living room drinking coffee. When the phone rang, one of the half brothers went into the den to take the call. He returned to tell us our father had died. We all embraced, and it was as if the scene stopped, a freeze-frame shot. It was suddenly very still; the only movement came from the sea outside, the waves breaking, and the brush of fabric as we hugged. Silent whimpers. He had died alone while we ate, the day after the wedding. I still don't know why he died alone, why my mother, who must have known it was the end, decided that we would eat dinner rather than sit by his bedside and hold his hand as his heaving gradually stopped.

"Kids, your father is at peace," my mother told us. She sighed. "Hope was gone."

The next morning, just as the caravan from Camden had arrived only days earlier, horns honking as they drove up the driveway to the house, two black limousines drove the same path, disgorging the family lawyer and his junior associate and in the following car a representative from the bank.

Our family lawyer wore a three-piece black suit, pinstriped, summer weight, his Phi Beta Kappa key on a watch fob in his pocket. His teeth and fingers were yellowed, a result, judging from the smell, of years of smoking, and his hair so greased it did not move, even in the breeze off the ocean. The banker and the two lawyers all carried briefcases. The junior associate was a young woman about my age who sat on an upholstered chair in the living room in a tailored suit and stockings, with her ankles neatly crossed, taking notes as the lawyer spoke.

The lawyer passed out copies of the will, and then he passed around pens with the law firm insignia along the side. He explained that it was customary that everyone sign something agreeing not to contest the will. He then passed us each a piece of paper with the signature line blank at the end.

He spoke about what "John" had wanted, as laid out in his will. John this, John that. It was a lengthy preamble to whatever he was going to read, and I found myself wondering how this guy in the three-piece suit with the yellow teeth and hands and my father were on a first-name basis. Or was that what lawyers and bankers do when they are preparing to read a will to a client's family. Set the family at ease? Or to imply they were so chummy that they knew firsthand what "John" really wanted? He also called my mother Pat, and she seemed to take that gracefully in stride. It seemed he was on the approved list for calling her Pat.

The will had only one surprise in it. Which was that, instead of distributing my father's wealth among his wife and seven children, my father left everything to my mother. Yet no one debated this at the time; we all signed quietly, obediently, all my father's children, as the junior law associate stood over us, one by one, to collect our papers, the block heels of her sensible pumps digging into the shag rug as the pen scratched along the dotted line seven times. My mother, on her side of the couch, sat smoking as we signed, one leg crossed casually over the other, blowing long trails of smoke into the still air as her eyes followed the junior law associate move around the room. Just outside, seagulls skimmed the sky, landing on the lawn, raucously squabbling at each other.

I wonder if birds talk like us, I was thinking as we were signing, *if they fight like us, and we just don't understand them.*

"I love you, I love you, I love you."

"How come you never tell me that?"

"I'm telling you now. I love you."

Maybe that's what birds are saying in their own language,

maybe they are having a lovers' quarrel and we just don't realize it. Maybe they are breaking each other's hearts over and over again in the blunt flat light of the midmorning summer sun.

Eventually the limousines departed, driving down the driveway into the second half of August. The tent from the wedding was down; the sprinklers hissed their arcs of mist over the lawn. The waves kept on coming. It was white flag at Georgica Beach down the way, meaning it was safe for swimming. There, young kids with boogie boards chased the surf, hurling themselves into the waves. Lifeguards took shifts sitting on the high wooden chair, keeping watch over the stretch of sand between the orange flags that delineated public-beach territory. The Good Humor truck pulled up to the edge of the tar parking lot, and a line of sandy children formed at its window, shifting from foot to foot on the heated tar as they waited their turn.

The very first summer we lived by the sea, the Army Corps of Engineers had hauled dozens of old, rusted VW Bugs onto the beach and set them upside down in piles along the first dune, just past Georgica Beach. Juan Trippe, the Pan Am founder who lived down the road, had ordered the Bugs to be formed into a makeshift jetty as a defense against erosion. This first attempt to save the coastline, to keep the line of shingle-style cottages on the beachfront between Georgica Beach and Main Beach safe on the coveted first dune, worked for a while. The sand gradually built up over the cars, and so the eyesore of rusted junk heaped on the gentle sand dunes disappeared. As children, we fantasized about the lives of families who had driven those cars long before they were scrap metal used to ballast our homes. We'd find a fragment of a bandanna, ragged, coarse pebbles and sand embedded in its knots, and keep it in a shoebox along with our shells and chips of blue and green beach glass. We'd imagine it was the bandanna worn on the head of the mother of a family who had driven out to the beach on a fine summer day. We made up stories about the family, where they were from and what they ate as they picnicked by the waves. They drove out in a convertible Bug, we decided, and they drove from the city for the day. Their car was yellow. They had a radio and they sang as they drove. Beach Boys music. Maybe one of the kids wanted to be a surfer when he or she grew up, and kept a secret pile of surfing magazines in a box at the bottom of the bedroom closet. Maybe the mother was pregnant again, and soon there would be a baby sister or brother. Maybe they were going to visit the grandparents. Maybe they had a dog.

Soon after they were first laid in the dunes, the VW Bugs were eclipsed by modern jetties, and the coastline where the strip of shingled cottage homes stretched out along the dunes appeared secure. The rusted Bugs, their service no longer needed, were to lie forever under the dunes, their existence known to fewer and fewer generations as time went on.

Walking down the beach that afternoon, I thought of a line of scripture from John. My father was John.

"Let not your heart be troubled," the scripture read. I walked past the rows of shingled houses, past the house of the neighbor who had pitched himself into the sea, down past the beach where, deep underneath, the VW Bugs still held memories of distant families long gone.

"Let not your heart be troubled . . . In my Father's house are many mansions: if it were not so, I would have told you. I go to prepare a place for you."

· X ·

The Franklin Stories

MY FATHER LIVED on in Franklin, in a box in my desk. The white legal-size envelopes with the barely legible penmanship, the stories typed on onionskin paper, the pages creased over time, the fold marks deep. If I wanted ever to hear his voice, I would open that box.

An Encounter at "Ralph's Rest"
By John I. B. McCulloch

It was a wet autumnal night in New York, and I had found no taxis available. Since my left leg (the arthritic one) was giving me an unpleasant time, I had managed to drop in at a few bars en route home to give my agony temporary surcease, before proceeding further.

It was at the third bar, I believe, that

I decided to risk a longer pause, and here I discovered two amazing things. One was that the name of the bar was "Ralph's Rest," which would seem to suggest a mortuary establishment rather than a hotbed of fun and games.

The second thing I noticed was my companion on my right. To describe him as a slithery creature would be perhaps an injustice, but this was the first adjective that drifted into my mind. In any event, we were the only two customers that Ralph had occasion to deal with that evening. The slashing rain that battered against the windows (its force had increased) was sufficient explanation for this.

As we were the lone patrons, I felt it perhaps incumbent on me to attempt a small conversation, particularly since, of the two of us, I was the only one in a virtually erect position.

"Have one with me? Can't fly on one wing, you know," I asked in my most amiable tone.

Then I glanced at my bar mate, and blurted out, "Oh, I say, I am sorry."

"Don't worry," he said wearily. "Happens all the time. But I do accept your offer."

"What will it be?" inquired Ralph, appearing suddenly from the wings.

"Eight scotches and sodas please," said our friend casually.

There is really not very much further to tell about this particular encounter. The rain

had abated, and since a young couple had just
descended from a taxi, my drinking companion—
having gulped down eight scotches—jumped into
the cab and indicated to the driver eight
different directions. The chauffeur departed
with a pleased expression on his face.

"Isn't that dreadful?" said the young lady,
whose name turned out to be Sheila. "He'll take
him to the Empire State, the Midtown Tunnel,
Shea Stadium, Bloomingdale's, and God knows
where else, and triple charge him. That's what
they do to these visiting octopuses."

"Octopi, dear," said her companion, whose name
was, I believe, Sir Rodney Stedly-Smythe, who
had apparently an almost morbid fixation with
classical plurals.

My Friend Franklin
By John I. B. McCulloch

Note: JJ dear, here is an installment of
Franklin. I finally managed it.

You're getting too old for my stories, but
as you keep asking for them, your wish is my
command. But this is the last one I believe.
With love and pride, Daddy

It was some three days after I had last seen my
new octopus friend entering a taxicab headed

in eight different directions that our paths
crossed again. I was on the same barstool at
"Ralph's Rest," since my left leg was still
aching, and no medical man in his right mind
would have recommended further physical exertion
in these circumstances.

My friend—whose name, he now told me, was
Franklin—drew up a stool next to mine, bringing
with him a rather bracing ichthyne odor (I might
possibly have coined this word). Franklin had,
it appeared, done a Cook's tour of Manhattan and
escaped a taxi bill for seven hundred and fifty
dollars by the simple expedient of going into
Bloomingdale's to buy a toothbrush, and emerging
out the other entrance.

Despite this triumph Franklin looked unhappy,
and after he had consumed twenty-four Scotches
(eight triples) I tried to draw him out.

"It's this damn social life," he complained. "I
may as well confess that I do not lead a totally
celibate existence. Theodora (the metropolitan
press insists on referring to her as my Constant
Companion) is a great one for giving parties.
Unfortunately, the CC is of my own species, with
certain minor but fundamental differences, and
she does not know her right flipper from her
left flipper (she has, you will understand, a
multiplicity of choices). Tonight, we are having
for dinner both the Chilean Ambassador to Upper
Volta, and the Turkish Ambassador to Outer

Mongolia, and how we're to seat them God only
knows."

Franklin ordered another round of scotches
(he had cut down to sixteen) and a reminiscent
look came into his eyes.

"Sometimes these things can be positively
embarrassing. Once Theodora inadvertently put
Dr. Walter Shadd, the eminent neurosurgeon,
next to Miss Virginia Rowe, the authoress. The
Shadd-Rowe combination caused our other guests
considerable merriment (without which we could
have easily done). And then, of course, there was
the case of Sir Gilbert Prawn, KGBHQ2QED, Her
Majesty's Ambassador to the United Nations.

"Ambassador Prawn," said Franklin, bolting
down a potato chip, "had had his eye for some
time on a young lady at the other end of the
table, a Miss Esmeralda Curry who (I later
ascertained to my dismay) was no better than she
should have been. When the butler arrived with a
steaming tureen of prawn curry, it was more than
Sir Gilbert could resist and he swept Esmeralda
(who was no better than she should have been)
off into a waltz. This would have been perfectly
correct, I suppose, except that the music had
not yet begun. In any event, Esmeralda shortly
suggested that they lie down, sorry, sit down,
I meant to say. I have never understood whether
it was the lack of music, or the fact that
Ambassador Prawn kept massaging Miss Curry's

left buttock with an enthusiasm worthy of a
nobler cause. Heaven knows how everything will
end up this evening. CC's parties usually result
in total confusion. The Chilean Ambassador will
probably land in Outer Mongolia and the Turkish
Ambassador in Upper Volta. Their problem, not
mine."

"One more round for the road, sir?" said
Ralph, the barman.

"Oh, yes, I suppose so," said Franklin, "but
only eight scotches this time. A wise man (or a
wise octopus) knows when to taper off."

· XI ·

Going Back

"FAMILY BUSINESS" IS what my mother called it. She said it to each of us over the telephone, my half siblings, my sisters, and me, the long-distance wires crackling. "It's high time we conduct our family business," she said. When she wanted something, she knew how to get it. We agreed to gather in New York in June, ten months after my father's death.

On the ride to the airport, everyone was wrapped in their own individual fog, staring out the window of the car as if the expanse from the Midtown Tunnel to JFK, the dull sameness of the highway, was the most interesting thing in the world to look at. Finally, my mother broke the silent ride. "My neck knows we're getting on a plane," she said. "It's already tightening up." Then she asked Keith, "How many pieces?" This was a line of our father's. It's what he would say before we arrived at any airport. He was a zealot on the art of travel logistics. He loved making plane reservations and planning complicated flight connections. He'd call any airline at least three times to reconfirm our seats. His favorite was the baggage claim, when we'd have up to ten pieces, including a medicine chest, and along the way a laundry bag our father checked through to the next airport. He had a hanging bag for suits, a trunk for books, and three leather suitcases that he'd fill only halfway, one for underwear and shirts, one for shoes and bathing suits, and one for "toilet articles"—hair tonic, his prescription medication, razors and brushes and the like. A good many family hours were spent around baggage claim conveyer belts over the years, waiting for bags to emerge, often with long, empty lulls between sightings. When his laundry bag broke, as was often the case, the entire family and a baggage handler and driver had to scatter the length of the conveyer belt, darting in and out of the elbowing airport crowd to snap up loose socks and stray boxer shorts. So, when my mother asked Keith "How many pieces?" I knew she was thinking of him. Then she added, "I wonder, should we check him?"

Keith had been put in charge of our father on this trip, and he'd been carrying his ashes all the way from the funeral home in Manhattan, where he'd gone to pick them up. Keith had our father in a white leather tote bag he'd brought from Florida for the occasion. He wouldn't let any of us look in the bag, not even to see what the ashes looked like. "He's in a plastic case," he said, "you can't see anything anyway," pulling the bag closer. Catherine wanted to move our father into her knapsack. "He'd die if he knew he was in a white leather bag," she told Darcy and me, but I couldn't figure out how we'd do it, and I was not sure he'd care. He wasn't a big one on clothing aesthetics; he just wore whatever our mother told him to, which was always blue. Blue suits, blue shirts, blue ties. "It brings out the blue in his eyes," she would say, which was surely true. When I thought of him, I thought of his eyes. How his eyes were a soft, pale watercolor blue.

We were traveling to a place only my mother remembered, but she thought the rest of us ought to too. A lake town in Switzerland called Lugano, where my parents spent summers when Darcy and I were very young and then when our mother was pregnant with Catherine. In her photo albums, Lugano is a rustic village in primary colors: sun-whitened stone houses, bright bursts of red and yellow flowers in window boxes and along walkways, smooth, curving green hills, and in the center a dark, flat span of blue lake. Darcy and I are in most of her pictures wearing matching monokinis, or matching sundresses, or matching T-shirts and shorts. In one picture, we are wearing large dark glasses and sun hats that hide most of our faces, each of us clutching a blow-up duck. Apparently, the half siblings came to visit once, arriving for a long weekend in a defiant knot. They insisted they had no memories of coming to visit Lugano, but my mother had the photos to prove it, a series of faded black-and-white snapshots of a picnic on the lake. "You were all in fine moods too, I can tell you. Real brats." Keith, Scott, and Rod must have been in their late teens; in the photos they are wild-eyed and clean-shaven, their bodies taut and brown.

As we approached the town, things started to take on a startling familiarity, yet the kind that comes when a landscape long stared at in photographs suddenly spreads out in real life. It was an empty feeling: things looked familiar, but there were no memories to punctuate them with. My mother, on the other hand, had a story for just about every street corner. "This is where you took your first steps," she said to me, pointing to a grassy triangle of park off the road. "Here is where your father and I would take a walk after he finished sitting around with his nose in a book all morning, down that road, by the lake. And here—here, kids, is where we'd stop for an aperitif on the way back up the road." She continued on, tapping the window of the car as we drove by a small outdoor café with red umbrellas and cockeyed wicker chairs. From the front seat, she looked back at us, half excited and half impatient, as if at any moment we'd all burst forth with recognition to match hers.

But all we knew is what we knew from what both she and our father had always told us: "When we go, we want to be together in Lake Lugano." A lovers' pact, made back when they were still lovers. When their life together looked long and unimpeded. "Let's be together for always."

I remembered something from Lugano. On my birthday, probably my third, I couldn't sleep through my nap, so I snuck out on a long terrace outside my bedroom. In my mind's eye, I see the yellow of my pajama feet against the cool white tile of the terrazzo floor and, off to a corner, a pile of pink and white birthday presents, delicate, cheerful, their slender ribbons swaying in the afternoon breeze.

My mother was using some of the money left to her by our father for this trip, and she made constant reference to the "estate." Maybe because of her sudden financial authority, we fell mindlessly into line behind her as we entered the hotel, following like a gaggle of ducklings as she led us up a deep red, thickly carpeted stairway to our rooms.

The Hotel Splendide was large, and glistened pink in the sunset off the lake, like a fairy-tale castle made of spun sugar.

Though it meant nothing to anyone but her, she had booked us into the same rooms we'd had twenty years earlier. She settled in a large suite with a view of the lake and put my sisters and me in an adjoining room she called the "baby-and-governess room." "MB and the boys," as she called them, were given smaller rooms across the hall with no view. Within minutes Keith was back in our room, pacing, opening window shades and bureau drawers. "I look out over a brick wall," he said, and slumped in an armchair.

Our mother was out on the terrace that joined our two rooms, a long white marble terrace with woven rattan bistro tables and chairs placed in pairs. She waved a "Bar and Room Service" menu in her hand. "None of this was here before," she said, pointing the menu at a cluster of apartment complexes and a casino across the lake. Mainly, she was talking to Catherine because, to her, Catherine was the only one who had not been to Lugano before. "Except she was once, really," she pointed out. "In my tummy."

My sisters and I stood on the terrace. In our mother's photo albums, there were dozens of photographs of Darcy and me posed there: in matching terry cloth bathrobes, in sundresses, in our nightgowns. In a few we wore Swiss nurse costumes someone had given us, with red crosses on the hats. On our necks, in the photographs, we wear stethoscopes. Catherine stood with us and watched the lake with her arms crossed, her eyes on the unfamiliar landscape. Sometimes, I knew she disliked being the youngest; if she could, I knew she'd find something in all of this she could remember.

"I remember the terrace," I told my sisters, but I never told our mother.

· · ·

One summer long ago, my parents must have looked out on this terrace onto the lake and vowed to each other that their ashes would be scattered in Lake Lugano. I tried to imagine such a conversation between them. Probably late at night, after dinner and maybe a dance down in the garden below to the music of the trio that played nightly, maybe they had one last drink on the terrace of our suite, sitting on the bistro chairs, gazing out as the lights across the lake in the houses on the hillside reflected in the water, their two small daughters curled in the bliss of innocent sleep in the adjacent bedroom. What in the protocol of love takes romance to this precipice, where decisions about death are made with an eye toward eternal union? Did they ever think, I wondered, during the years that followed, when their backs stiffened and strained and gradually bent over time, when they grew ever distant, when disappointment became an ache, a blindingly thick overlay to everything else, did they ever in moments remember, *We have this pact, we're in this together for eternity*? I liked to believe that they did.

At dinner that night, my mother wreathed us around a table on the hotel veranda under a web of tiny lights. As we were seated, she greeted waiters as though they were long-lost dear old friends. "You probably remember these two from when they were babies," she said, pointing to Darcy and me. "*Bambini!*" one crooked old waiter cried out and nodded. Another went back to the kitchen and returned with an elderly woman in a housekeeping apron. A small woman, her face wizened but her eyes bright. She clasped her hands to her cheeks when she saw us. She came and gave us each a kiss on both cheeks. "*Lo ricordo,*" she said. "*Sì. Sì.*" *I remember. Yes. Yes.*

As we ate there was music, a trio of musicians in white tie and tails. Keith had been taking a series of hustle lessons in Florida, and he danced with each of us while his brothers watched. As he danced, he coached. "One two three, one two three," he whispered in our ears, and "We're turning here," before he held his arm out for a spin. I didn't mind it, but it drove my mother crazy. "Come on, Keithie," she said, stopping in midglide. "I wasn't born yesterday, you know."

When we were young, our father used to dance with us, holding us out at arm's length and sweeping us across the floor, the pleats of our dresses flying up behind. Often, when people saw us dancing, they beamed. They'd come over and ask our names and our ages. Sometimes they guessed wrong and called him "grandfather." When my parents danced, though, he up on his toes most of the time, she gliding into his steps with grace and knowing, head held high, no one asked questions. They watched.

"It's one of the things that made me fall in love with your father, girls," our mother used to tell us. "He was such an elegant dancer."

"Oh, honey," our father would add whenever she said this, "it takes two."

Maybe that was what marriage was, I often thought. Dancing together. If I could freeze that moment. My parents on the dance floor: a surety and synchronicity of step, so that when one moved backward, the other moved forward to meet them there, reflexively, confidently knowing where their partner was at all times and following where they were going. That's what marriage ought to be, at any rate, the perfect marriage everyone aspires to. A long and intricate dance between present and past, moving always together in step toward the future.

The morning in Lugano was bright and warm. Outside the
bedroom window the hotel was already a clatter of movement.
China clinked in the restaurant below, and car horns blew on
the narrow side street.

A soft lake breeze brushed past us as we filed down to the
hotel dock at noon. When we got there, there was a motorboat, picnic lunches, and a pile of yellow beach towels waiting
because, my mother decided, if we're going to be out on the
water anyway, we might as well make a day of it. "Technically,
it's illegal to do what we're doing here," she had explained to
us the night before at dinner. "It's considered littering, putting
anything foreign in the water. The Swiss have very strict pollu-
tion laws these days, and they're proud of them. The driver will
look the other way if we make it look like he's hired to take us
out for a day's picnic. I 'greased his palm,' as your father would
say, so he'll be fine." Then she looked at my sisters and me.
"Girls," she said, "you have to remember this, because you'll
be back here again someday. With me."

The hotel had packed easily enough food for twenty of us—
sausages, cheeses, fruit, wine, bread, sparkling water in blue
bottles—all packed into white plastic garbage bags that fluttered, in the breeze, like a flock of nesting gulls. Somewhere
along the line, Keith transferred our father in among the bags,
tucking his white leather tote bag in alongside a shiny ther-
mos of coffee and a basket of fruit. When our gear was loaded,
we climbed tentatively one by one into the boat, all knees and
elbows as we shifted around to get settled. The driver was a
young man with muscular arms and reflective aviator glasses.
"Do you wish to eat first?" he asked.

"No, no. After," my mother said, busily arranging a wadded-up towel between the side of the boat and her lower back. Then, "*Allons-y*," she said, turning to all of us, her mouth zipped into a tight grin.

When the boat rushed out of the dock, in a sudden dart, it shook us from our sleepy dazes and whipped away our breath. Bouncing across the lake, we had the wild, light-headed feeling of being scooped up by something fast, something powerful, something practically out of control. As we picked up speed, the lake opened around us, curving, snakelike, between hilly villages on both sides, past squared-off acres of farmland, past stone churches and tall campaniles. "Ten years ago," the driver shouted over the motor, "the lake was so polluted they had to dredge it. Now," he said, "it's clean again. Really, really clean. After lunch," he added, winking at my sisters and me, "water-skiing!"

When the boat came to a stop, we were in the middle of the lake, and the scenery on either bank looked like everything else we had passed. In the sudden silence of the cut motor, though, we heard birds singing, and far away a bell rang in a church tower, or on the neck of some wandering cow. For a moment, we all turned our heads this way and that; then slowly we dropped our eyes down and stared at our knees. Keith fished the gray plastic container out of his white tote bag and walked to the back corner near the motor. Beside me, trying to be quiet about it, Rod cracked his knuckles. Our mother had her head down, one hand supporting her forehead. "Unh," she said once, a deep, dark sound from somewhere inside her, but no words.

Balancing himself against the rim of the boat, Keith held the container carefully over the edge. From where the rest of us were seated near the driver's seat, all we could see was Keith's back, and his elbows jutting out at angles from his waist.

For a while, there was the familiar noise of water slapping methodically against the boat and the occasional rustling of plastic in Keith's hand. No one spoke. After a while the rustling stopped. There was that certain buzz of quiet that comes when sound loses meaning.

Part Two

· XII ·

The Visit of Holiday Whales

CAMDEN, MAINE, 1986

THE CARD WENT out a month before Christmas. It was a holiday card—that much was immediately apparent due to the red envelope. The photograph on the front of the card was a line of smiling faces in jeans and sweatshirts. Behind, a rugged mountainous landscape cut the cloudless summer sky.

Inside the card, Raymond Jackson had typed up his annual holiday newsletter. It was printed on red paper and folded neatly in quarters to fit inside the envelope. Helen had gone down to MacBride's on Main Street to have it copied a few hundred times. It was going out to everyone on their list, all the friends and relatives who liked a greeting at this time of year. Helen liked to make a lot of lists, and the Christmas list was one of them, an ever-expanding work in progress over the years.

"Dear folks, hail and hello from the Jackson family on High Street," it began.

*It's been a booming year for all of us. I've had a steady run
in my work and fun. The boat publishing business continues,
and on the leisure side, Helen and I got out on the water
for four days in August with our kids on a double-ended
schooner. Went all over Penobscot Bay last August with
Dean and his bride, up from New York City. She goes like a
dream. Hoping one of these days these kids will produce some
boat-nut grandkids for this old fud to teach some sailing to.
(Hint hint, kids!)*

   *We're looking forward to having all our kids home for
Christmas, as well as Helen's mother, Nonnie. Raymond Jr.
will be coming from Seattle, with his fiancée, Claire. Jessica
is coming in from San Francisco, and Chris will be in from
the Farm (the University of Maine in Farmington, for all
you out-of-staters). We hope those of you nearby will drop in
to toast the season! Helen will be making her usual arsenal of
traditional holiday cookies. To those far away, you are nearby
in our hearts always. To all we send our best wishes for 1987!*

                    With our family's love, as ever, to yours.
                    Helen and Raymond Jackson,
                    Christmas 1986

Helen had studied calligraphy at Skidmore, and she addressed each card in her careful script. "People like things per-
sonalized," she said. "It never fails to make an impression."

"You know, I read these things and I want to throw up." My
mother was smoking on her side of the couch in her living
room. The Jackson card had arrived with the morning mail on
her breakfast tray a few weeks before Christmas.

"I just had to call you and vent," she told me. "I mean, really. It kills me, to think that a child of mine is caught up in this."

What bothered her about it was the lineup, specifically my presence in it. "What is a daughter of mine," she said, "that's what I'd like to know, what's a daughter of mine doing in someone else's Christmas card. It doesn't seem natural somehow, I'm sorry. There I've said it. I've said my piece."

But she hadn't yet. Her piece. She wasn't done saying it, and she was digging right in.

"I mean, 'folks,' please. Your father would roll in his grave. Using 'folks' that way is tacky, dearie, plain and simple. It's 'folktale,' 'folk dance,' 'folklore,' fine, permissible. But not as a form of greeting. People are not 'folks,' they are people. Their tradition is folk. 'Folks,' no. I've always told you children that. And now here you are, caught up in it."

"In what, exactly?"

"*It*, dearie. You know full well what I mean. You should be home for Christmas. Not gallivanting off. With some other family."

I could hear the draw of her cigarette. My mother managed through years of practice to get her smoking to take on expression. This was cigarette smoking in "I just had to call and vent" mode, the indignant inhale, the agitated exhale. Her smoking repertoire was as changeable as her mood. There was dreamy, nostalgic smoking, in which the exhale was long and lazy and the atmosphere thick with anecdote. There was busy smoking—economic quick puffs in rapid succession—or busy with no hands free, speaking on the phone and writing, say, or sorting through place cards for a party, in which the cigarette was held in a clench between her lips. Then there was brooding smoking, the deep inhales and the long, whooshing exhales. Finally, there was dramatic smoking as proclamation, lighting a cigarette, rarely putting it to her mouth but instead waving it like a torch as she made a point or two, letting the ash grow long until it listed to one side and eventually fell off. Even extinguishing a cigarette had meaning. It was an energetic stub, repeated any number of times until the butt was thoroughly smashed in the ashtray. The most energetic of stub-outs usually accompanied the "I just had to call and vent" repeated smoking she did around the time of the holidays ever since I'd been married to Dean. Always, the filter was stained a deep red by the end of it all from her lipstick.

"Trust me, baby girl. Idiomatically, we don't speak the same language as those people. Did you even see this picture before it was sent? It's odd."

Actually, there was something somewhat odd about it. Perhaps it was the uneven terrain, or the tilt of the camera, but it seemed as if everyone in the Christmas card photograph was standing on an angle, leaning in on one another as though if one dropped out, the family pose would entirely collapse. At the center was Helen, in a pink sweater and matching windbreaker. The Raymonds, Senior and Junior, were on either end of the lineup, as if bracing us in.

"To think," she said, "that a child of mine. Jesus."

A week before the trip to Camden, my sister Catherine and I were in my kitchen in New York, trying to make marzipan. We agreed I needed to bring something with me to Camden as a present. Something. We had taken food coloring and mixed it in empty mustard jars. She shaped hers into oranges, bananas, and pears. I was making whales, because I knew Dean's family liked whales even though I couldn't be sure they liked marzipan.

I was telling her about the sleeping arrangements in the Jackson household during the vacation. "Dean and I have to sleep in the master bedroom," I told her as we mixed colors with the ends of tiny paintbrushes we'd bought at the hardware store. For some reason, the sleep arrangements were what was bothering me. "Raymond is staying on the pull-out in his study, and Helen is staying in her guest room at the top of the stairs, in one of the twin beds—Chris is sleeping in the other."

"Why him? Why not the girl?"

"The girl refuses. Jessica." My sisters refused to remember Jessica's name; they had no room for another sister in my life, even an in-law sister.

Catherine's tongue poked out slightly from her mouth as she worked. "I'm really not half bad at this, you know? I think we may have stumbled on something."

"Jessica is staying on the couch in the living room, and Nonnie, the grandmother, is staying up in Chris's room. No one knows what the fuck to do with Raymond Jr. when and if he arrives with the fiancée. They are fighting over whether to get married or not, and they might not even make it. She's got cold feet. They're coming from Seattle and they're planning to erect a tent to sleep in."

Catherine was not big on camping trips. "She's gonna have more than just her feet cold in that case," she said. "That West Coast girl's going to have some icy you-know-whats."

"They are setting it up in the attic."

"Well, we'll call at regular intervals and check in on you," Catherine said.

I brushed elaborate eyelashes and red mouths on my whales. I wanted sensuous whales at the family gathering.

Catherine watched.

"These whales," I said as I worked the brush, "if nothing else, these whales are going to get through this thing with grace and style, even if it kills them."

Catherine laughed. "And they are killer whales."

In Camden at Christmas, there were annual town rituals. During the week of the holidays a "living crèche" was enacted on the green outside the library, so if you drove up from the south, you'd see actual town residents wearing long burlap robes over their parkas, gathered around a makeshift manger. Organized by the Congregational church, the "Congo," the shifts were four hours long, pending weather. Originally the holiday committee borrowed livestock from a farmer in Hope to round out the nativity scene, but that had changed a few years earlier due to a runaway sheep. The sheep tore out of the manger, up the road, jumped off the dock outside Cappy's, and drowned. A papier-mâché menagerie made by the church guild over the summer was pressed into service ever after.

Someone from the Congo always called the Jackson household right after Thanksgiving to see if any of the three boys might be coming home. The three would make perfect wise men, the Congo organizers annually agreed, especially if one or more had conveniently grown a beard over the year, as one or more invariably had.

The day after Thanksgiving, wreaths with red velvet bows were hung on all the lampposts along Main Street. Dodge Everett, who ran the car repair store in town, dropped in to pick them up at the Women's Collective, where they were handmade. Weather permitting, they remained up until Twelfth Night, when Dodge came by in a battered pickup truck to take them down. The routine of this tradition relaxed the town around the bustle of the year's end; it was a predictable rite and as such could be counted on when often nothing else could. Yet everyone remembered the year a freak ice storm scattered pine and ribbons all over the harbor two days before New Year's. The sudden mess unnerved the whole town until gradually the last of the flotsam of greenery and ribbons rode out silently into Penobscot Bay in the dawn of the new year.

There was also the traditional reappearance of the town's young people, those who had left Camden to go on to college and jobs elsewhere and returned home for the break. Up and down the street, as Dean and I did our Christmas shopping, people stopped to greet him. "Mr. Foul Shot!" one man called out across the street at us. "Back in the flesh!"

Sometimes in the middle of the night, when Dean couldn't sleep, his hands would jut up in the air, making mock foul shots in the dark. In those moments, I knew whatever was bothering him, he was calming himself down by working his way back from his present to his sweet past.

When it came to local sports, Dodge Everett, also the high school basketball coach, was a well-thumbed almanac. "How about that game in Lincolnville—'75, I think it was—when you guys really showed them how to play hoops?" Dodge said. In the chill of the December afternoon, he and Dean making clouds with their breath as they spoke, Dodge counted out the scores of winning games on his gloved fingers. "You come by and see us, Dean-o. Sure would be a thrill for the kids, having you show up at team practice one day. Local hero and all."

He looked at me and winked. "Mr. Foul Shot, he is. That's our boy." He punched Dean in the arm. "Come on by and see the old gym. Give the kids a thrill."

"Honey, I hear you ran into Dodge in town this afternoon," Helen said. We were at the dinner table. Red candles glowed in the candelabra. Nonnie made little figurines out of red yarn that she called Cossacks. They lined the mantelpiece and the sideboard. In the living room, they dangled off branches of the Christmas tree like doomed mountaineers.

Dean's brother Chris poured wine into the cut glass goblets. He creased his brow as he poured, careful to keep the measurements equal, the bottle held just over, never touching, the rim of each glass. "I'm perfect at this," he said. "A real sommelier."

At the head of the table, Raymond Sr. was carving the lamb. In the kitchen Helen poured the drippings into a gravy boat, shook mint jelly out of the jar. "Dodge's wife, Josie, called to tell me he'd seen you, honey," she said as she walked in.

"I saw Nelly James," said Nonnie. Nonnie was ninety-one. She had been celebrating Christmas with Helen and Raymond since they had married thirty-five years earlier. When her husband, Lester, was still alive, the two would drive up from their home in Westerly, Rhode Island, together. Now she was widowed, and Chris always drove down from college to retrieve her. She sat at the foot of the dining table in a pale purple sweater suit. "Nelly came by to have tea with me. I was busy, what with the Cossacks to finish and all, but we had a nice chat."

"Nelly came by to have a nice visit with you, Mother," said Helen, setting the gravy boat down at her husband's side of the table. "Drat." She swept up some overflow with a finger and licked it.

"Jesus, Mom," said Chris. "Do we really need your spit in the gravy?"

"That Nelly James never misses a chance to come by and poke her head in," Nonnie continued.

Helen held out her hands and smiled across the candles, across the bowls of vegetables, across the roast, to her husband. In the candlelight, Raymond's bifocals were flickering shields of glass.

"Can we do a toast?" she asked.

Everyone groaned.

"We're just getting started on this grub here, Mom," said Dean.

Helen took the hands of the two sitting closest to her, her mother and Dean. "Now. I just want to thank you all for being here with me this year," she said. "It always means a lot, but for me, this year, it's just very special." She looked around at her family. "We're family, first and foremost. I'm very grateful for that and I thank you all."

During the visit of the boat, the summer before, Raymond and Helen had first told us they were going to have a trial separation. Four days on the double-ended schooner in Penobscot Bay, where there was nowhere to run, they decided would be a good chance to claim our undivided attention. One night, the night before we set sail, I thought I heard Raymond coughing, followed by a light step that creaked the floorboards down the hallway to the back stairs. Fingers dialed the phone by the half bathroom; then the receiver hung up. But it may not have been Raymond at all but rather the after-drizzle of a dream: noises imagined in the vulnerability of half sleep. I would lie on my back a long time in the still house, Dean's breathing steady beside me, until I heard breakfast sounds. It started with classical music on the radio. The refrigerator door would open, then shut. But no smells, no other sounds. Because breakfast was not toast, or bacon, or anything that smelled like Helen's usual cooking those summer mornings. And you could not hear cornflakes getting their milk splattered on. At least not with my ears.

As we sailed out of the harbor the following morning, the hills over Camden were soft and purple against the dark blue August sky. Helen put her hands on her hips and breathed in the sea air. "Purple mountains majesty," she said. "You know where those founding fathers got that idea if you look back at our town."

Raymond adjusted things, pulling at sails and re-coiling ropes. Occasionally he asked Dean to do something and they worked in tandem, barely a word between them. Gradually the busy community lost definition and melted into a blur, the white steeple on the Congregational church the last focal point, shrinking smaller and smaller, finally just a toothpick, then gone altogether as we bounded out.

We anchored in the cove in the evening and for dinner we ate lobster, tearing at the bright bodies, tossing the shells over the side. Dean skimmed a lobster tail across the smooth water. It didn't skip exactly, but made a few shaky ruptures on the surface before it sank.

"A lousy substitute," Dean said to his father.

Raymond shrugged. "You've gotta try everything." This was Raymond's motto, handed to him from his stint in the Camden volunteer fire brigade. "When you don't know what you're going to need," he'd say about whatever, "roll everything."

"Honey, you need another sweater?" Helen asked me.

"She's always cold," said Dean.

"Oh, I know, she's our city girl," Helen said. She sat on a boat cushion, the kind with two handles, for easy throwing to overboard victims. She stirred sugar into a mug of coffee. The steam swirled, misting her face so she looked like a silent-film heroine. "Still, honey, I think you could use a new one. Let me make you one for Christmas."

Since Helen had knit me the red claret sweater during the visit on the lake, I wore it every visit I made to Camden. "I bet you could have fun with this, dear," she told me as she fitted it to me, stretching a tape measure along my back as I held my arms out in a T.

"Anyone, anything else?" Helen asked. "Anything hot?"

There were times I regarded Helen almost as an exotic animal, her behavior both fascinating and strange. A life made up of unconditional offers. Fudge, sweaters, hot drinks.

"Pizza," said Raymond, "if you're calling out."

"Cute, Daddy," Helen said. "Daddy, real cute."

But that was not what marked the visit of the boat. It came later, just barely twilight.

"Mom and I have something to say," Raymond said. Dean and I were lying up on the cabin roof, side by side on our stomachs; below us Helen and Raymond sat in the cockpit.

"We're going right down the line with this," Raymond said. As he said it, his right hand cut the air in front of him. The line was Raymond Jr., Dean, Jessica, then Chris. Whenever Helen and Raymond had something important to say, they announced it in order of birth.

"We phoned Raymond Jr. yesterday," Helen told Dean, almost apologetically.

"So tell then," Dean said. "What's the big news?" Dean hated it when Raymond Jr. knew something he didn't.

Raymond looked down at his hands, and so did everyone else. Everyone watched Raymond fold his fingers in on themselves, then open his palms, then close them again. Then he opened his palms once more, straining them back, letting all his fingers wiggle at once. *Here's the church*, I was thinking. *Here's the steeple.*

"The fact is," Raymond said. He looked up at Helen with a slant half smile, then looked down again. "It seems I have fallen in love with another woman."

Helen put her hand on Raymond's back, then withdrew it. For slow preposterous seconds, no one spoke. For starters, the idea seemed absurd. Raymond in love. Raymond with his gold bifocals, his skinny little legs. Raymond romancing? Raymond Jackson in love?

It seemed too awkward and potentially nauseating to ask for details, besides which, after Raymond spoke, Helen started to cry. Quiet whimpers, sniffles mainly, her chin resting on her fist. I realized I'd never heard Helen cry. Usually a laugh was her guard for everything. A lusty head-thrown-back kind of whoop that pushed everything else back inside.

"'Seems'?" Dean said. "As in, you're not sure yet? Seems you have fallen in love, Dad? Really? 'Seems'? That's the word you're going with? Come fucking on."

"We haven't made any permanent decisions yet," Helen finally got out, wiping her eyes. "We're going to give it 'til Christmas, right, Daddy?" She groped for Raymond's hand and he let her have it. Pink parka, pink fingernails, pink face.

"This is pretty disgusting," Dean said after a while. He shuddered.

"What do you mean, honey?" Helen asked. "I don't understand." She asked him pleasantly, as if she had just asked him to explain long division.

Dean went on. "Look at you, Mom. Sitting there like a fucking wounded animal. Dad, I want to kick you in your back, straighten out your posture, man. What the hell?"

"Okay, fair enough," Raymond said. "You've got a right to be mad. I am okay with that. I deserve that." He looked up at me. "I want to know what our city girl thinks," he said, his eyes blinking calmly.

What did I think. They were supposed to be predictable—not like my parents, where potential surprises lay behind every waft of smoke, every can of Budweiser—and to want the same things. That had always struck me about Raymond and Helen. There was never any vying over decisions, or if there was, no one knew it. They moved as one complacent force through a lifetime of card games and homemade sweaters and cheese sticks.

A million words floated in my head. A million random,

useless words. "I don't know. You guys always seemed so perfect to me." As I spoke, Helen nodded, sniffling. "Well, I guess now you seem more normal."

Helen laughed through tears. She grabbed a lobster shell that had fallen to the bottom of the boat and tossed it over her shoulder. "Normal!" She turned and patted her husband's knee. "That's a new one, isn't it, Daddy?"

Raymond cast his eyes out to sea, as if looking for something, a fin, a periscope, anything to distract us with. Family time was supposed to be happy time.

"I don't know," Helen said. "Maybe I'm crazy, but I'll tell you this." She gave a long blow into her tissue. "If I had to do it all over again, I wouldn't change a minute." She smiled, her eyes wet and bright. "Not too many people can say that, you know?"

As soon as the photos from our wedding were sent to Camden, Helen and Raymond looked at the images of themselves and had a reaction. *I should have worn a darker blue*, Helen thought. *Dark hides more, it's more forgiving to a figure. I can't possibly be that heavy.* Raymond thought, *I should get contact lenses, those gold-rimmed specs make me look like an old grandpa. I can't possibly be that ancient.* They ordered no copies of photographs of just the two of them. Soon after this, they started taking a journal-writing class at the local Y in Camden. "Do a little something new," Helen said. "Bring in a little spice back to the old marriage," Raymond added. It started as a kind of experiment, a therapy exercise. All the couples they were friendly with in town were doing some form of therapy, and they were eager to try. In class, they were asked to keep a notebook and to write in it every day. To write down whatever came into their mind, for forty-five minutes. Raymond usually did this in his den. Helen preferred the living room, listening to classical music on the stereo. They followed the class instructions carefully. Put it all out there, the instructor encouraged the class. See what you can learn when you set pen to paper and let your mind roam where it will.

Helen wrote a lot of lists. Shopping lists, Christmas lists, wish lists, a To Do list and a Not To Do list. "This is one of the things I have to stop doing," Helen wrote on the Not To Do list. "I have to stop speaking for Raymond. I have got to stop assuming I know what's on his mind. Because I don't. I obviously don't."

"The things I miss most" was another list. "Cigarettes, my brother Bob (Bob was killed in World War II), summers when the kids were young, my father's clambakes on the beach, sometimes, Homer Winfree." But she changed that last one. "No, the idea of Homer, not Homer himself." Homer had been the boy who came to court her while Raymond was off in the war. Homer had asthma and couldn't go to the front, and spent the long Sunday afternoons of the war in Nonnie's kitchen making light conversation and accepting the women's offers of tea and cake.

Raymond wrote about a lot of things. His family, his friends, his kids. He wrote a lot about expectations. "I would like to do something I'm proud of, something on my own." The words "my own" came up a lot. "I love Helen, but I need some time away from her," he wrote once. "I'd like to be more on my own." Again and again, the same phrase was repeated, practically word for word: "I need some time alone." Finally, Raymond told his notebook about Cathleen. "There's this girl in my office. Well, not a girl, a woman." Cathleen was just forty. She had straight dark hair and wide-set eyes. For years, she told him one day, she had had a crush on him. She liked his gentle manner and his easy gait. Now they were having lunch together, taking their separate cars to a diner in Rockport. The first time, he was just back from the wedding in East Hampton. He told her all about it. About having to have the rehearsal dinner clambake under the tent and not on the beach as planned (the caterer was not up to Grampa's standards, he added), and about the tennis matches by the cottage. Then he told her about John McCulloch having a sudden stroke. "The guy just up and died, like that," he told Cathleen. "Daughter's wedding. One minute there, and the next, breathing with a ventilator in the next town." Cathleen's eyes widened. "I don't want to go like that," Raymond told Cathleen. "It really makes you think. Started me thinking, anyway." Cathleen nodded. She patted Raymond's hand. "I'm so sorry," she whispered across the table as he drank his chowder. "Life is short," Raymond told the notebook. "Sometimes you have just got to seize the day. It could have been me, hooked up to machines. You never know what's going to hit you." He told that to Cathleen. "Seize the day," he told her, as they guiltily spooned up chowder at the Rockport Diner. She nodded. Outside the nip of late fall was in the air. Soon the first flakes of snow would dust the harbor town. Suddenly, Raymond confessed to the notebook, he was thinking about Cathleen all the time.

"Confidence," Helen wrote on her wish list. "I feel like such a boob all the time. Raymond says nothing has happened yet between him and Cathleen, but he thinks he might be falling in love."

"I feel like an adolescent," Raymond wrote. "Or, that's its springtime." But he crossed out "springtime"—"(Too cornball)," he wrote in the margin as an editorial note to himself. Over the winter and into the next spring, Raymond and Cathleen followed their now familiar routine along Route 1 to Rockport, or sometimes all the way to Wiscasset for ice cream. He would drive first, leading the way; she'd follow, waving to him at stop signs so he'd see her happy face in his rearview mirror. It made his day, those glimpses of his junior associate in the rearview mirror of his car heading to the diner with him. "Maybe it's a phase," Raymond wrote in his notebook as spring turned to summer, and summer again into fall. "Do I hope it's a phase, or don't I?"

"Will things ever be the same again?" Helen wrote. But that launched her into another list. "People I can't forgive: My mother, for crying all the time, over everything." When word came that Helen's brother Bob was dead, Nonnie cried so hard it's all Helen remembers of her adolescence. A small once-resilient woman crumpled by grief. "Bob, for dying. I always thought we could have gotten along." Helen was a male-oriented woman, she always said. When the "hard core" of Camden used to get together, it was Helen who always joked around with the men while her friends Nelly and Jan kept to themselves. "Raymond. Yes, Raymond Jackson too," Helen wrote on her list the week we were due to arrive in Camden for Christmas. "I'm finally getting really ticked off about this." But when Raymond was around, Helen was eager, attentive, like a schoolgirl with a crush. "I thought I had been doing everything right," she wrote. "But I must have been doing it wrong."

"I can't let him go, I can't let him!" she wrote one day before all her children were due to return home for Christmas. "All I care about is him!" Then, "I hate myself like this," she wrote the next.

"How's it going?" Catherine asked, calling halfway into the Jackson family dinner. She called from our mother's apartment, where they were having the annual Christmas Eve gathering. I dragged the kitchen phone cord around the corner and hunched on the back stairs.

"So far, so good. But the shit's about to hit the fan, I think."

"Well, you hang in there. We'll call later, after the Wall family have taken their sugared-up children and gone home. Lou Anne Wall hit the bourbon pretty hard tonight, before it went into the milk punch, and now she's singing that song about beans and rice and coconut oil again."

The phone cord swayed back and forth, a silent pendulum. My mother picked up on another extension.

"Dearie, is it you? Jesus, that girl has got to stop."

"Who?"

"Lou Anne. Lou Anne Wall. She's my dear friend, but she has no voice. I daresay she's terrifying Johanna in the kitchen.

"Ma, everything terrifies Johanna," I said.

"Never you mind. You're not here. So. Tell all. How's by you?"

"Nothing to tell. We're having dinner."

"I see."

"And so far, that's about it."

"Un-hum. I see."

She waited.

"Ma?" said Catherine. "They're having dinner. Shouldn't we get off?"

"Whatever." She sighed. It was the wistful sigh that often preceded the nostalgia cigarette, and promptly I could hear her lighting up.

In the dining room, they were calling my name. "Yoo-hoo," Helen called out. "No dessert without the daughter-in-law!"

"Ugh, I heard that, dearie." The first exhale of the cigarette ended up not being her nostalgic/wistful slow one but her scoffing/indignant fast one. "Jesus."

There was a loud trill in the background. "Jesus, someone shut that girl off," my mother said into the extension. "Catherine, be a dear and unplug Mrs. Wall so there can be Peace on Earth this holiday season, will you please? Tell her I have something to show her in the library. That will distract her."

When Catherine rang off the line, my mother said to me, "I don't like it, dearie. I don't like it one bit. That family is trying to pretend everything is nice and normal when that father is cascading, in full view of you all, into a midlife crisis."

I thought of Nonnie's Cossacks on the Christmas tree, hanging by a thread to a branch. Raymond Jackson, hanging from the family tree, willing himself to let go.

Only Nonnie didn't know what was going on. She knew a bit of it. She knew that Helen and Raymond had been having some problems. Helen had alluded to it on the phone. No one had yet told her the full extent: that Raymond had rented an apartment in town and that for the entire autumn, until he returned a few days earlier with a pillowcase of laundry and another filled with presents, Helen had been living in the house alone. And only

Nonnie had no idea about the other woman, Cathleen, whom he thought he might be in love with. No one had met her yet, this Cathleen, no one but Chris, who had returned a book years ago to his father's office when she was the receptionist. They all agreed, all the kids, that didn't count, because nothing was going on yet, and besides, Chris couldn't remember a thing about her except dark hair.

What Raymond and Helen didn't know was that after dinner, after Nonnie had been put to bed, the kids would call a family powwow and demand that the air be cleared. "I will not spend a week up there pretending we are one big happy family," Dean's sister, Jessica, had insisted, "when we're not. When that's just about the last damn thing we are."

"So thank you all," Helen said, finishing her toast. "Thank you for coming home."

Raymond Jr. and his fiancée, Claire, were flying east from Seattle, where he had been living for ten years and where they met in a group house on Lopez Island. In October, he'd given her an ultimatum: marry me, or that's it.

Raymond Jr. was a nester, he kept telling Claire, kept telling everyone else. "Look," he'd say, "you're not getting any younger. You know?"

Ever since Dean had gotten married, it had been weighing on Raymond Jr.'s mind, marriage. He hated it when Dean achieved any developmental milestone before he did. On the way east on the plane, Claire and Raymond Jr. had had a fight. "Look, I'm not saying I don't want to be with you," Claire said. "It's all so public, getting married, though. All these people I don't even know asking me what kind of china pattern I want. Who says I want china at all in my life?"

"Okay," said Raymond Jr. "Forget the announcement, forget the china." But Raymond Jr. never knew when to stop. "Let's forget the whole thing," he said next, and for the rest of the trip, the plane ride, renting the car in Portland, the ride up Route 1 to Camden, Raymond Jr. thought about it. Bringing his fiancée home after years of imagining it. First he was excited; then he was furious. All this time he'd been telling himself, telling Claire, what a perfect marriage his parents had. "Marriage doesn't work," Claire would say. "It's not a natural situation."

"No," Raymond Jr. would tell her, "wait 'til you meet my parents. Thirty-five years, and still happy." *Goddamn Dad*, Raymond Jr. was thinking, driving up the dark roads along the coast. *Asshole*.

Raymond Jr. and Claire arrived at the house a little after 8 p.m. Everyone rushed out to greet them at once, warm and smelling of fire smoke and wine. Only Nonnie remained at the table, spooning extra sugar into her teacup, blinking in the candlelight.

"You're just in time," Jessica told her brother. "We're calling a powwow as soon as Mom puts Nonnie to bed."

"You have beautiful eyebrows," Nonnie told Claire when she was brought to the table to meet her.

"Come on now, Mother," Helen said, grabbing Nonnie by the elbow and helping her up. "Bedtime."

Nonnie's legs were like thin matchsticks, poking out from her kilted skirt. Every Christmas someone in the family would give her a pair of running shoes for support, but she never wore them. She insisted on her patent leather pumps with square heels like blocks. She walked up the stairs in small steps, her hand gripping her daughter's arm. "That's it, Mother," Helen said, pushing her lightly from behind.

The family settled into the den, arranging pillows, carrying mugs of tea and kindling for the woodstove. Helen brought in a glass platter filled with Christmas cookies. There were all her traditional ones: the coconut-rolled rum balls, the almond macaroons, the jelly wafers, and the chocolate bark, plus a few dried-out marzipan whales with long eyelashes and red lips.

"Hey, Mom, slide those rum balls over here," Jessica said. She was lying on the floor by the fire, one leg resting on a knee.

"I'm having one of these delicious whales," said Helen, plucking one with a forefinger and thumb. She chewed. "Cute," she said.

"These your whales?" Chris asked me.

"They're marzipan. You have to like marzipan."

"Take 'em," said Dean. He took a handful of chocolate bark off the platter. "I'm not much of a marzipan man myself."

For a week, Helen had been baking Christmas cookies. They sat in tins and boxes in the storage nook by the back staircase. All week, she worked at it in the kitchen alone, filling the empty house with the smells of baking. "It will be like any other Christmas," she told herself, told her "hard core" friends Nelly James and Jan Brice.

"Be careful, Helen," they'd warn her, but Helen, with the holiday music already playing on the stereo, hardly seemed to hear her friends.

"I'm so excited!" she told me over the phone. "Waiting for everyone to come home. So *busy*."

So busy, just waiting.

"I guess I better start this thing off," Raymond said. He sat in his plaid La-Z-Boy by the fire. He tipped the chair back and forth softly. Usually, after dinner on Christmas Eve, the Jacksons were in separate bedrooms or in the basement, busy wrapping presents. Chris and Dean would sit in their childhood room, still covered in basketball pictures and banners, and pick out songs on the guitar. Jessica liked to rummage through boxes of old letters and books she stored in the attic. She liked to take a glass of wine up there and get softly tipsy as she unpacked her past. Then, at 10:30, everyone put on scarves and coats and drove down to the candlelight service at the Congregational church. "Hitting the Congo" was a Jackson family tradition.

"So, start things off," Raymond Jr. said. "Let's hear what you have to say, Dad." He crossed his arms. In Seattle, Raymond Jr. had almost completed his training to be a family therapist, and this was his big chance to show off to the family. "So, Dad, let's hear it." His hands tucked deeper into his armpits.

Raymond Sr. glided two fingers over the empty ring finger on his left hand. He glided over and over, looking at the fire in the woodstove. "I guess Mom has kept you all pretty up to date on what's been happening here," he started out. "And I'm grateful for that." He looked in her direction and she nodded back. "For the past few months, Mom and I have been living separately. But we both wanted me home for Christmas, with you all. We both very much wanted that." Raymond looked over at

Helen's face, and she nodded again. The logs hissed and sparked as they burned.

"To: One and All," Helen's letter had said. "From: the Old Squaw of Camden."

She had written the letter to her children the day after Thanksgiving, right after Raymond had told her he wanted to think about a divorce. She had written it and gone directly to MacBride's on Harbor Avenue to have it xeroxed four times. "Daddy and I are talking about Xmas plans!" the letter had started out. "We're both so thrilled to think of all our young people making the big trip home!" Then the letter had a smiling face, followed by, "Just today, they put the wreaths up on Main Street!"

The second paragraph went, "Daddy and I haven't seen each other much this fall, but every day, I feel his presence in me more and more. What we have together is very strong. I think he knows that, and I want all of you to know it too. We will always be a family!"

"Oh, family policy," the final paragraph read. "Everyone bring home five little presents for the giant stocking. And no duds, Chris!" The family stocking was a large red wool sock the length of a leg and the width of a torso that Helen had knit back when the kids were in grade school. It was passed around on Christmas morning and one by one the family took presents out, only replacing them if they had been the ones to put it in. The stocking was passed until it was empty, and everyone had a collection of little presents and wads of discarded wrapping by their sides. The last time the Jacksons had all been home for Christmas together, all Chris had put in the stocking were matchbooks and rubber bands, all neatly wrapped in emerald green tissue. "I love you all!" Helen concluded. "From, a very excited Mom!"

On the bottom of each individual copy, Helen had added personal extras. "Chris, honey," she had written to her youngest, "no matter what happens, I will always be your mother." On Raymond Jr.'s she had written, "I look forward to having Claire in our family group." She added nothing to her daughter Jessica's copy. I imagine she tried, that she stood in the copy shop holding her pen high over the letter, but that no words came. "Jessica's such a grown-up girl," she often told me with a sigh. "I don't even know how to talk to her anymore." In the copy shop, she might have thought that and then wondered, *Have I ever known how to talk to her?* Dean's copy had one simple word in small letters across the bottom. "Help" is what Helen wrote.

"Well, Dad, I've just got to ask you," Dean said. "You've been married thirty-five years, and you think you can just walk out on it?" He looked up and caught his father's eye. Raymond Sr. nodded at him to go on. "I think you're a real wimp."

"I think you're a jerk," Jessica said. "And I'm damn pissed."

Helen and Raymond had always encouraged honesty in their children. "My kids call a spade a spade," Helen had boasted to her friends Nelly and Jan again and again. "Raymond and I are always so astounded at how much they pick up."

"A total ass-wipe," Jessica added.

"I have a question for you," Raymond Jr. leaned back in his chair, his arms still tight against his chest. "Have you two considered a marriage counselor?"

"No," said Raymond Sr. to Raymond Jr. "No, kiddo. There just doesn't seem to be any point."

"But there is a point, honey," Helen said. "I mean, we could look back, reexamine." As she spoke, her hands began to move, rising in circles around her. "Find out what went wrong, what we could do better. Plenty of people have great success with the new techniques." She looked at her eldest son. "Don't they, Raymond Jr., honey?"

"No. I guess that's not what I want right now," Raymond Sr. said.

"Now?" Raymond Jr. asked. "Or ever?"

"I don't think so." Raymond Sr. bowed his head. "Wow, that's not so easy to admit," he told the floor. "Wow."

"Think so, *what*?" Helen asked.

"Mom, Jesus." Jessica spoke from the carpet. "Get with the program. Listen to what the guy's telling you. He wants out." Jessica looked up at her father. "Doesn't anyone understand English around here?"

Jessica and her father had already had this discussion. "Jess, I'm calling to tell you, I'm going to divorce Mom," he had said. He had called her at work the week after Thanksgiving—she was the only one. He'd tried to meet Dean when he'd been in New York for a sales meeting in early December, but Dean had been out of town and never returned the call. Raymond Jr. was too far away, and Chris—he and Helen wanted to spare Chris as long as they could.

Jessica had just come back to her office from a lunchtime aerobics class. Her desk was piled high with messages and faxes. "I'm trying to quit smoking, and he goes right ahead and hits me with this," she told all her siblings over the phone. "I mean, what the hell? Does he think calling me at work is a great way to tell me he's fucking some chick and ruining our family?"

"What do you have to say about it, Mom?" Dean asked. "No one ever thinks to ask Mom. Does anyone else see this besides me?"

Everyone suddenly looked at Helen.

"Go, Mom," said Chris, "your turn," as if it were her turn at charades.

Helen drew a deep breath. "Raymond Jackson," Helen started, because whenever she had something important to say about her husband, she always used his whole name. She folded her hands on her lap. "Raymond Jackson is at the very core of my existence." She smiled weakly.

"That is ridiculous," Raymond Jr. said. He shook his head. "Sorry, Mom. Wrong answer. No one is the core of someone else's existence."

"What a lot of horserot this is!" Jessica yelled. "I can't stand it."

"See?" said Raymond Jr. "Feminist no-no. We're talking feminist no-no here, Mom."

"Wait, I don't think she said 'the core,'" I said quietly to Raymond Jr. "I think she said 'at the core.' There's a difference."

"That's right!" Helen waved a finger at me. "Our city girl's got it."

"It's still ridiculous," said Jessica. "He's a dishrag, Mom. The guy's a loser. Look what he's doing to this fucking family."

From the La-Z-Boy, Raymond Sr. spoke. He rocked back and forth easily in his favorite chair. His fingers gripped the armrests. "I think we've done enough calling of names around here, folks," he said.

"Damn," said Raymond Jr. It was one of the things he was trying to get on top of in family-therapy training: don't let it digress to name-calling. "Did you just catch that?" he asked Claire. "I blew it."

Claire sat beside Raymond Jr. on the loveseat in silence. As she listened, she twirled the edges of her long ponytail between two fingers. Her silver-framed glasses made her look very wise, but also very distant. Raymond Jr. also wore his brown hair in a ponytail, though it was a short one that flipped back up in a curlicue around the base of his neck.

"I don't think," she said to Raymond Jr. in slow, measured words, "you're supposed to tell anyone they have the 'wrong answer' either, honey. And they've been name-calling this whole conversation. You only just heard it."

The phone rang and Chris grabbed it. "Jackson family psych ward," he said. "We specialize in nuts in ruts." He listened. "Oh, yeah. Hi. Of course. She's right here." He mouthed to me, "It's your mom."

Helen put her head in her hands.

"Saved by the fucking bell," said Jessica. "Thank God. Let's stop this nonsense and get out the eggnog. It's almost time to hit the Congo."

"What *now*?" the familiar voice hissed into the telephone. In the background, carols played on the stereo in my mother's living room. "O Holy Night."

Evidently Mrs. Wall had gotten into the bourbon again. "Night deeviiii-yun," Mrs. Wall merrily wailed.

"Are they holding their voodoo sessions again up there?" my mother wanted to know.

"You got it," I merrily replied.

"I can't stand it. I've said time and again, you don't do these kinds of things without a professional present, dearie. You mark my words. Something is going to blow up."

"You just may have a point there, Ma."

"Something is going to blow sky-high. I just don't like that a child of mine—"

"I am a grown woman, you know, Ma."

"Not to me you're not, you never will be, so there. Mark my words on this one."

"It's Christmas," said my sister Darcy on the extension. "We love you!"

"Much love to everyone up there except that bastard father, behaving the way he is. Sweet and kind, everyone thought. So ha to that! And 'folks,' dear god, he says 'folks.' I'll leave it at that. It's too much, girls."

"Peace on Earth," added Catherine.

Mrs. Wall rang out in song. "Deeee-viii-yuuun . . . O night, O night deeevine," her voice insisted.

At the door, Dean crossed his arms. He was already in his parka for church.

"Mrs. Wall is singing," I explained. I held out the phone so he could hear.

"Cathy," my mother whispered to my sister on the phone, "the woman must stop her singing. She doesn't have the voice. It's like a ruptured duck. And in my household. No one bothers to tell her."

I missed them. They were my team. My small army of women. The living room would be warm, the radiators ticking. Platters of salmon on black bread, and small disks of caviar on toast. Outside, the lights on the Christmas trees would shine all the way down Park Avenue. The smells would be deep cinnamon, evergreen, and clove, and Mrs. Wall would be in the foyer in a velvet muumuu, stationed under the mistletoe in the door frame, a goblet of milk punch in her hand, bright pink lipstick staining the rim of her glass, her eyes looking off dreamily at the chandelier as she sang.

"I have to go, you guys," I told them. "It's time for the service at the church."

My mother let out a short laugh. "First, they sit around insulting each other, then they go pray." She lowered her voice. I could hear the exhale of her cigarette smoke. "I simply can't stand a daughter of mine involved."

"Ho-ho-ho," my sister Darcy put in.

"A fine Christmas, girls," my mother added. "Jesus Christ."

Heading toward Main Street but turning off, away from Route 68, the road soon became sparser. Slowly the bed-and-breakfasts and smattering of houses thinned out. The Camden Hills lay to the left, silent in the darkness. It was a clear night, and the lighthouse on Curtis Island stood sentry just offshore. The Christmas candles in the windows of the lone estate on Hound's Tooth Head glowed as we passed. As the road away from Camden narrowed, it curved into the farmland on Appleton Ridge, where a young man named Jerry Grantham had been killed two years earlier when his truck skidded on glare ice late one winter afternoon.

"He should have had chains," Jessica said. She had waited for me, the others already headed to the Congo in Raymond's station wagon, all except Raymond Jr. and Claire, who had stayed at home to erect their tent in the attic and go to sleep. Jessica made an elaborate detour, driving the upper hills in Helen's car so she could secretly smoke. She opened all the windows in the old Volvo. Whenever I went anywhere with Jessica, the most mundane acts suddenly seemed illicit.

"He was the type, though. Typical Jerry, not to have his chains on before the first storm. He was one of those big mountain-guy types, always most comfortable out of town. I think he always thought the woods would protect him. But they figure he died instantly. So that's something. He was less than a hundred feet from the barn he and his fiancée, Lynne, had just fixed up. Lynne was at home, and, according to Mom anyway, at least an hour must have passed before a car passed by and found the truck upturned."

We passed Lynne's barn, where a few lights were on. Jessica flicked an ash out the window. "I never liked that girl. I know things haven't slid easily for her, but what a moony-eyed dope. You should have seen her in high school, the looks she used to give Dean. Big cow eyes. Really dumb too. Cow eyes and cow hips."

The things Jessica hated were simple: women who got her brother's attention, stupidity, and fat. "Good thing Dean found someone in my image," she said. By which I assume she meant a bitch. It was Jessica's highest form of praise.

The Congo was pearl white with candles in each window. People filed in in hushed tones. By the side of the vestibule the Jackson family was waiting, held back because Helen insisted we all walk in together as a family. A mother of sons, she knew how a boy jammed his hands in his pockets, the weight of his distraction. The Jackson boys, at church, waited just so, their scarves loosened and parkas unzipped, leaning against the plaques

along the sidewall or pacing silently like caged lions. Jessica
had always been a single unit until I came along, shy in her
way, uncommunicative, without conspirators. Now there were
two of us. "Two females" is how Helen referred to us. "We
have two females in the family now," she'd say to her friends,
as if she'd been looking at a chromosome readout. Helen knew
it was silly at this age to expect it of us, but she nonetheless
expected some curveball, some theatrical sort of rebellion. She
didn't know what, but she had heard her friends Nelly and Jan
speak for years about the trouble with raising sisters, and so despite our age she kept on her guard. It wasn't anything she had
had experience with. Maybe we would giggle in the sermon, or
trip getting into the pew and expose our lingerie to the Congo
congregation. She had had only brothers herself, and so she
recognized the behavior of her sons, the way they drank milk
out of the carton in front of an open fridge, the years of smelly
sneakers and sports equipment cluttering up the hallway, the
grateful way they ate everything she cooked. Like Jessica, she
was used to being the only girl in a family of boys. Her anxious
look, as we entered the church, made us both clasp our hands
over our coats and walk solemnly, eyes on the floor, following
the boys up the aisle to the pew.

At the end of the long aisle, Helen waved and signaled to
various people. Raymond leafed slowly through the hymnal
open on his lap. Dean sat with his hand in mine; occasionally
he scratched one finger lightly against my knuckles. Then the
organ began the processional carol, "Adeste Fideles," and everyone rose. With the music, the small community of people
standing in long rows of family joined together temporarily,
in honor of the holidays, in song. They sang unevenly, some

louder than others, some softly, as if unsure of the tunes. Some spent the time with their heads averted, watching the others. Beneath the complex pattern of wood beams on the church ceiling, the ancient room swelled with their secrets.

"I'm the one married sixty-six years, longer it would be if Lester was still alive, so don't think I don't know a few things."

I sat with Nonnie in the guest room at the top of the stairs, the voile curtain playing against the wall as Helen's portable floor heater blew warm air into the room. Nonnie was teaching me how to make her Cossack dolls out of knitting wool. Her bony hands worked slowly as she spoke.

"I know this," she went on. "People are always looking for the answers. There's only one answer when it comes to marriage. You have got to make it stick."

It was clear she was practiced at making the little woolen men, her Cossacks, who dangled off the branches of the Jacksons' Christmas tree each year. She barely looked down at her hands as she worked the yarn.

"There were plenty of times I could have gone off, or Lester, but what were we going to do then? I ask you. Isn't it all about family? About family sticking together? You know it is. You give out all the pieces of your heart. And then there's always more to give. This old heart would be long gone now if that wasn't the truth."

As Nonnie spoke, she looped a black piece of yarn around the middle of the red to make the first Cossack's waist sash.

"I remember like it was yesterday," she told me. "No. Not even. Like it was just this very morning, just today, that I first saw Raymond Jackson, the first time he came a-courting Helen.

He was a handsome boy, I'll tell you, a good looker from the start in that spanking-white US Navy uniform of his. You went weak all over, looking at them in their uniforms in those days. It was summertime, he came to our house in that Navy getup of his, and I knew he was one of the good ones. Good Yankee blood. I thought he understood. But you never really understand the way a man's mind works, don't even try. You know that, right?"

She looked up at me. "Listen here, they don't even understand it themselves," she said, "most of the time. A woman's mind is different. Here, hold this for me." She gave me a ball of red wool and drew a strand of yarn out long. She looped it around her forefinger and thumb. Age spots mottled the fine white skin of Nonnie's hands, yet her fingernails were long and gleaming. "We all want to pretend it's equal now. Women and men. Well, it will all be equal in heaven. Down here, a man's mind is still going to be a different matter no matter what amendments get passed. We have rights, yes, but we'll never be able to change a man's brain and whatever's in there, well, I'm not asking. I'm not pretending to know. A strong woman keeps her own counsel, I always say."

A whistle blew just then, from downstairs. After a while Jessica appeared in the doorway, in her leotard and leg warmers. She had her hair in a ponytail and a sweatband around her forehead.

"I'm getting ready to start," she told me. "And you are my pupil."

Nonnie looked her granddaughter up and down and clicked her tongue. "Well, look at you, Jessica. You don't have any clothes on." Then she amended that. "Except socks."

"Class is starting," Jessica repeated.

"You go ahead," I said. "We're kind of in the middle here."

"We're artists at work," Nonnie said. "You can join in, Jess, if you put some clothes on."

"I'm off," Jessica said. "I'm also at work."

Jessica was teaching a fitness class in San Francisco, and over the holiday she was working on her routine. On most afternoons in the Jackson living room, she and I would prance and stretch amid the furniture and holiday decorations. She shouted instructions and I obediently followed. After, we rested with tea.

Nonnie looked at me after Jessica had gone downstairs. "Such a lovely girl, I don't know why she wants to look like a skeleton. But here, where was I. Hold that light up, will you, so I can see to get the necktie on this little fellow."

She took the red yarn and yoked one side with a strand of black. She tied a knot and snipped the extra while I held the gooseneck desk lamp down over her handiwork.

"The important thing," she went on, "is, even if you could understand a man's mind? You can never see inside of anyone else's marriage. Not really. Certain things never show up when you're on the outside looking in. The wallpaper on the inside, I mean. The fine design."

The wallpaper on the inside, the fine design. I thought about that. How do we put up the walls that define our marriage; how, over time, do we etch the fine design?

"To be honest," Nonnie said, "I didn't see Dean as the type to marry a city girl. Maybe Chris. Chris has an eye for the fancy. He's the only one of the boys to ever notice my ring. 'Oh, Nonnie, that's so beautiful,' he told me."

She held up her left hand. The ring she'd worn over sixty

years was a narrow gold band, a diamond braced on either side by a small sapphire.

"Chris was only nine when he said that, and already an eye for expensive. My diamond ring. So it will be for Chris when I go, it will be for his girl. But Dean, Dean has always been content with the little things. Yes, that's why I didn't really understand why he was so taken with you, to be honest. 'Oh, she's a country girl at heart,' he told me about you, first time he brought you up here to Camden. 'Trust me.' But I wasn't so taken in. There you were with your New York City ways. That tuna salad you made with the French name and the anchovies."

"Niçoise."

"And your mother in those fancy leather pants when I first met her—green leather pants! I'd never. I could have sworn they were plastic. They looked like garbage bags. 'Trust me, Nonnie,' Dean told me. And like I told you, far be it for me to question what someone else sees on the inside."

She smiled. "That's why the pictures I save from weddings are of the table settings. At your wedding, I sent Chris down to take the shot while everyone else was up by the house getting seated before the ceremony began. I always want a shot before anything gets soiled, when it's all still fresh. To me, your table setting is real art, the pink rosebuds, the gold-rimmed plates. I have the photo on the sideboard in my dining room, right next to the one from Helen and Raymond's wedding. Maybe you can't see inside anyone else's marriage, but a photo of a table setting from a wedding, now that's the true art, it lasts forever. Okay now. Hold your hand up for me, help make one of these guys with me."

She looped red yarn back and forth a number of times,

between the forefinger and thumb of my right hand. "Hold steady," she said. "I'm going to put his little belt on now." She took a strand of black yarn and pulled it tight around the yarn in the middle section between my two fingers.

"So," she went on, "I'll tell you something every young married girl like you ought to know. The 'what if' principle." Her voice was at a register barely above a whisper. She leaned in toward me, over the electric heater. "You don't know what I'm referring to, right?"

"I don't know, that's right."

"Okay so. Did I happen to mention Jacob Fairfax to you ever? No? Never? I thought not. Jacob was a boy who grew up in Westerly, a few streets down from our house. Our families knew each other, from church and whatnot. Jake made a good living, he had taken over his father's country store when he was just barely twenty. He came to get me for a ride one day when I was just about eighteen. He must have been close to twenty-five when he came calling. My father nearly had a fit—a boy, a young man by that time, coming to get his daughter for a ride in a motorcar. What I remember is his coat, it was a nice brown tweed, and his red mustache. Nothing ever came of it. He deposited me back at home, and I remember my father hollering for a bit. I imagine he had a few salty things to say to Jake Fairfax behind my back because Jake never came back again, he went off into the day and left his memory behind. I was wearing my blue wool hat that day, pale blue like a winter sky. The following year Lester came home from the Great War, and we were engaged soon after that. But whenever I see a blue hat like that one I wore as a girl when I was out on the road with Jake, I think, *What if . . .*

That's all the cheating I ever did. My memories of Jake Fairfax and the motorcar ride. Just the what-if."

"The what-if."

"We all have them, don't we. The what-ifs."

"I suppose we do." I thought of Eliot Andrews, and for a
fleeting second, I wondered what he was up to. *What if.*

"I like to think it's a purer kind of cheat," Nonnie said. "The
what-if. It grows old with you, keeps close and as fresh as you
want it to be. No one can touch it, and no one need know. That's
how we did it in my day, because what would we have done,
Lester or me, going off on a hoot with somebody or other. No
way to get beyond it after that. So Lester need never to have
known that for sixty-six years, the memory of Jake Fairfax in
his brown coat with his cranberry mustache was in our bed
with us. Sure, a girl's got to have a little something on the side.
Just make sure the side is in the mind. And in the meantime,
you make it stick. That's the only secret to marriage, mark my
words. Make it stick."

Patch as much as you need; it doesn't hurt.

"I want to say something," Raymond Jr. said after dinner.
We were back in the family room. Chris was playing with the
plastic pins on the map above the couch. It was a map of the
world. The family stuck pins in every area where one of them
had traveled. Each person had a color. Up until recently, Raymond Sr. had been winning with his green pins—all his boat
races, cruises over the years, and then European junkets for
conferences. Since Dean and I had gotten married, his yellow
pins were populating most of Western Europe and bits of Af-

rica, the Caribbean, and the South Pacific. There were many struggles among the siblings about this. Chris, who had been to study in Spain, was the most vocal. "Just because *you* have been there," he'd say, looking at me but speaking to the group at large, "doesn't mean Dean qualifies to automatically stick his pins in."

"But they are a team," Helen would say. "That's the point. The marrieds are a team."

"You and Dad have been married since Christ was born, and you aren't a team," Jessica would argue.

"We are a team, honey," Helen would say. Looking over at her husband in his La-Z-Boy she'd add, "Right?" and nod her head.

"Oh my god, Mom, stop." Jessica, who was in her favorite spot in front of the woodstove, rolled over on her back. "Stop forcing yourself on the man. I can't bear to watch it."

"It hardly matters, Mom hasn't been anywhere anyway," Raymond Jr. interjected.

"It's a dumb game," Chris added. "Let's just stop it. Let's stop it right now."

The yellow pins came up whenever the Jackson family had guests visit over the holiday. They would ask about my travels.

"I just went as a kid, with my father when I was young."

"She speaks French," Helen would point out. "Our city girl has spoken to African tribes."

"I can't believe this," Chris would say. "Mom, get a life."

The guests were always perplexed. "It's not necessarily true," I would say. "My father was there learning Swahili, is all."

"Is *all*?" the guests would ask.

"See?" Helen would say. "Swahili! Have you ever?"

"I learned a few words, 'lion,' 'elephant,' that sort of thing. But it's not like we were living in the bush or something." I'd shrug. It all sounded absurd. "We were driving around in a zebra-striped minivan," I'd add.

"A zebra van! Have you ever?" Helen would insist. "She could have been stampeded by elephants."

"This is irrelevant," Jessica would say. "Let's hear about Alaska for once." One summer, Jessica had studied with a dance troupe in Anchorage.

"Or Spain," Chris would put in.

"Elephants can kill," Helen would go on. "The mothers, to protect their young, they stop at nothing. They did a whole segment on the *National Geographic* show. Hard to believe, but true."

Dean had put yellow pins all over East Africa, which was really exaggerating, and South Africa, which was a total lie. I had never been to the South Pacific, but there were yellow pins in Tahiti and Bora-Bora. Some days I thought, *What if I just took all my little yellow pins and went home? What if?* The little boy in the Masai village still played in my mind from time to time. Tied to a stake outside the family hut, a long rope around his ankle, naked and in tears. Sitting in the Jackson family living room, the wood fire crackling and the frost on the windowpanes, I wondered if that child was still alive and, if so, what he was doing. He'd be a man, with a family of his own, carrying water from the lake across the dusty village in the sun.

"Family powwow time," Raymond Jr. said. "I have something to say." He spoke to Chris, "Stop messing with all those pins and sit down."

Helen reappeared in the doorway with her platter of cookies.

By this time in the vacation, the cookies were pretty well picked over. Powdered sugar, shards of grated coconut and crumbs. A few dried rum balls and parts of my whales remained. She looked down. "Oh, dear. Pretty sad showing," she said.

Helen frowned, looking down at the platter. Then her face brightened. She snapped her fingers. "I know, I've got it!"

"Why don't you make a little fudge?" Dean asked.

"I was going to offer to make some fudge," she said. "What if I do? Fudge? Kids?"

"Forget it, Mom," Raymond Jr. said. "I have something to tell you."

"Sit, Helen," said Chris. "Take a load off."

"It'll take two seconds," Helen said. "It's a mix, I just add water and an egg and stir."

Raymond Jr. looked at his mother. "I think everyone knows what my beef is," he said.

"I don't know why everyone in this family has to have a 'beef,'" said Helen. She sat. "What? What beef, dear?"

"I was born while Dad was in the Navy, right? Right, Mom?"

He waited for his mother to nod. "Yes," she said. "There I was, all alone. Expecting."

So excited. Just waiting.

"No, once I was born is what I'm looking at. So here I am, the first baby. Getting all this love and attention, you know? How long, Mom? How long was it just you and me?"

"Three months," Helen said. "Three months almost to the day."

"Right. Then he comes home. Suddenly, boom. Mom has no time for me. Then they come along." Raymond Jr. looked at his siblings. "Boom, boom, boom. Three strikes and I'm out.

No one has ever had any time for me. As far as parenting is concerned, I am always the one left out in the cold."

"Now, Raymond, honey, that's not how it went," Helen said.

"See that?" Raymond Jr.'s voice raised. "I don't even have my own name? They three all got their own names. No, I'm just Raymond the small. Raymond the insignificant. Three months I was Raymond, and then into the shadows I crawled for time immemorial."

"Raymond, honey," Helen said.

"Yes, Mom, I remember being in my crib," Raymond Jr. said.

"This too is horseshit," said Jessica. "No one remembers being in their crib."

"I do," said Raymond Jr. "Highly intelligent people do, it's proven. I could probably remember getting my diapers changed if I thought hard enough about it." He tapped his temple.

Jessica rolled over and sat up on the rug. "No one remembers these things, Raymond. It's you crazy therapists who try to get people to remember things that never even happened."

"I remember being six," Chris said. "That's my earliest memory. I remember my little snowsuit." He looked to his mother. "The red one?"

Helen smiled. "With the blue piping. You were so cute. A little packet of dimples, you were."

"A tiny bundle of boy," Jessica said from her position on the floor. "Little Kiss-Kiss. Chrissy-poo."

The light off the fire zigzagged across the wall where the competitive map was framed. It zipped shadows across Asia and sparkled on Australia. The Northern Hemisphere burned with the kind of glow reserved for ghost stories around bonfires.

"Let me put this another way," Raymond Jr. went on. "I was at the salad bar at our local health food store the other day?"

"Is this relevant?" Jessica asked.

"Please. I was standing there, trying to pick the chunks of broccoli out of the pasta salad, when a voice came on the radio. The health food store always plays the talk shows with the science segments. They were discussing the rights of gay couples, but that's not the point. The point is, the commentator was saying, 'Does anyone know how to define the word *family*?' I put down the tongs and thought, *Shit. She's right*."

Raymond Sr. took off his glasses and started cleaning them with his handkerchief. "I'm getting old. That's all I know."

"Daddy's getting old and I'm getting fat," Helen said cheerfully.

"And I'm getting exhausted by all this," said Jessica. "How about that?"

"I am so disappointed in you guys," said Raymond Jr. He shook his head. "How can you be this way in front of my fiancée?"

"Oh, Ray, please," Claire said. It was the first she had spoken all night. "Don't use the word 'fiancée,'" she said. "It sounds so melodramatic."

"That's exactly right," said Jessica. "That's just what we are. Nothing more than a cheap WASP melodrama."

"At least at the movies, they serve popcorn," said Chris. "I thought I heard someone say something about fudge."

"That's it," said Helen. "Thank you, honey. I'm going to make it right now."

"Mom," said Raymond Jr. "Please. Stay." But she disappeared out the door, a slash of color.

Please. Stay.

. . .

On the bottom of the family letter Helen sent prior to the holiday to each of us, on my copy, at the bottom, she had written, "I think I'm lonely." But at first it didn't look that way. She was writing in script, the letters close together, and it looked more like, "I think I'm lovely." One letter changed, and she would go from lonely to lovely. Though both sounded foreign, absurd.

There was only one day left of vacation, and then Raymond would leave along with the rest of us. He had arrived like one of the children too, with a pillowcase of presents and a bag of dirty laundry. She kissed him the way she did her boys, holding his chin in one hand and looking into his eyes. Then she looked away. He had always called her Mother around the kids, but now the irony was not lost on her; it hobbled her. Her children had begun to take on the shapes of strangers, growing into their own lives, coming and going like shadows on the wall that didn't stay but appeared here and there sporadically and then passed. She couldn't piece together their various rhythms, the lives they lived without her now. Chris was supposed to be the last bird out of the nest, not her husband.

"I'm bummed out," Raymond had said to Dean and me that morning when we were having coffee with him in the dining room. "After you guys all split, Mom will be on her own."

Raymond was learning new words. "Split" was one of them. "Bummed" was another.

"Not our job, Dad," said Dean.

"Couldn't you two, at least, stay over for a day or so? Dean, you know Mom counts on you. Please. Stay. It would mean a lot."

I imagined Helen up in her sewing room off the kitchen, listening to this quiet conversation. To her husband's low, conspiratorial voice, planning his escape. *Please. Stay. It would mean a lot.* I thought of Nonnie just then. The way she would clutch Helen's hand at the dinner table to get her to stop clearing dinner dishes and listen to whatever story she was telling. *Please. Stay. I require your full attention.*

On the ice it was different. The water in the lake had frozen a deep plum color, almost black. The afternoon sky was clear. Jessica was doing figure eights, carefully balancing on first one foot, then the other. The loops got bigger and bigger; then she'd skate to another part of the lake and start again, first making very small loops, then gradually letting them grow. Her hands were in fists when she concentrated; her eyes never left the ice, set on the thin trails of a pattern she was carving out for herself.

It was the last afternoon of vacation. Chris raced across the lake in pursuit of a hockey puck. He and Raymond Jr. and Dean had been hitting it back and forth. Claire did not want to skate. She sat on a stump near the edge, reading a book, a scarf double-wrapped around her neck and head. It was a welcome present from Helen; she escorted Claire to the yarn store as she had done with me and let her pick out her yarn. Claire chose a reddish-brown rust color Helen called "burnt sienna" that showed off her blonde hair.

Across the ice, the puck raced toward me. I closed my eyes and swung the stick along the surface. It made a scratching sound but missed the puck entirely. "Keep your eyes open," Dean called. "You can't hit a dinosaur's dick with your eyes closed."

"Yo, Raymond," Chris called out, having intercepted the wayward puck.

Dean headed left in a fast skid to block Chris's shot. "Pay attention," he called out behind him to me. "You're the only teammate I've got out here, sweetheart."

He missed the block and his brothers scored another goal. From the stump Claire clapped her mittened hands. I lost my balance and fell.

"Oh, sweet jeez," Dean said, skating over to my side. He raised his hands to make the sign of a T. "Time-out, can I get some backup here? Jessica, get your buns over here."

But Jessica was concentrating on not being one of the boys, I knew that. Even if her lazy loops were boring her.

"Two on one, then," Chris said. "C'mon."

Dean and Raymond Jr. were skating hard, passing the puck back and forth. Their faces went serious when they played. Between shots, they would stand very tall, gliding, taking long breaths; then they'd focus, bend lower, and shoot. Chris made one quick circle around the lake, then joined them.

The game changed. The skating got faster, the shots fiercer; the boys huffed, making clouds with their breath. The sun dropped slowly toward the tip of Mount Battie. The afternoon mottled.

Another car pulled up beside Claire. She looked up from her book and realized it was Raymond. Now all three family cars stood in a row beside the frozen lake. "Oh god," Dean said. He whistled to his brothers. "Fud alert."

Raymond moved slowly from the car. He was in his parka, with his hockey skates draped over one shoulder. His car was packed up with all his belongings, the pillowcases full of clean clothes and his new Christmas presents. He had promised Helen he would leave first, before the kids, so she could have one last night alone with us. A game of hockey would be a good way to sign off, he must have decided, rather than do it in front of Helen at home. We all worried what that good-bye might provoke. And no one wanted to be dragged to his new apartment for a housewarming. Even he admitted he didn't want to make anyone deal with that yet, his brand-new one-bedroom rental in a development just at the base of Mount Battie. We were spared.

In the cold air, Raymond squinted. "You guys doing two on one?" he called out to his sons. "How 'bout a real game?"

"Yeah," said Dean. "C'mon."

"Show us what you got, Dad," Raymond Jr. said. He skated by the rim of the lake, scraping his stick behind him. "C'mon, I'll take you on."

At the side of the lake, I unlaced my skates. Jessica joined me. "It's getting too cold, anyway," she said. "Let's get Claire and take a walk around the lake."

On the stump, Claire shrugged. "I'm game, it's getting too dark to read anyway."

In the cold air, the world seemed broad, but the woods hung close. We set off on the path around the lake, the dry branches snapping under our feet.

"It's almost a mile around," said Jessica. "So if we do the whole thing, tonight we can have dessert."

Claire laughed. "I've never thought that way in my life," she said. She had small hands and feet, small hiking boots and red socks. Docile and compact. Jessica wore calf boots with a small heel. She teetered as she walked.

"Appearances," Jessica said. "It's all about appearances where I live and work."

From the ice, we heard a cry, then silence. We headed back

to the lake. The boys were in a circle on the ice. Raymond lay below them on his back.

"Holy chili peppers," said Claire.

"What'd you jerks do?" Jessica asked, wobbling down through the trees in her boots. "Kill Dad?"

"I guess I got him in the forehead pretty good," Raymond Jr. said. "Puck just went flying."

"I'm okay, bunny," Raymond said. He tried to prop his head up.

"He's fine," said Dean. "Just a head wound." Blood was spreading out of the gash on Raymond's head onto the ice. "Though we're going to have to take him home to Mom. Here he is with his pillowcase of getaway supplies, and we have to bring the little runaway back home. Won't she love that."

Raymond lay on his back on the ice. In the dark, his children were tall shadows above him. They stood with their hands on their hips. Trees. Conquerors. A solid mass of judgment.

"I'm fine, I'm fine," Raymond said. "No one worry."

When we left, the next day, Raymond had returned to his new apartment, his head bandaged and his road ahead uncertain. Helen stood in the driveway outside the family home alone and waved as we turned onto Route 1. She had given him compresses and ice packs and he had left. He was gone.

> *I think I'm lonely. One letter changed, and I would be*
> *lovely. What would that be like?*
> *I'm fine, I'm fine. No one worry.*

At the rehearsal dinner under the tent, Raymond's toast had been the highlight. He had produced a letter Dean had written

his parents once, when he was about ten or eleven. Raymond
had saved it all these years, he told the group, for this very occasion. Dean's rehearsal dinner. He held it up for all of us to
see, a child's handwriting on a simple piece of lined paper torn
from what appeared to be a school notebook. Dean put his hand
to his forehead and shook his head, smiling at his father. Raymond held one of the votive candles up and read it aloud, the
candlelight reflecting in his gold-framed glasses. "Dear Family," the letter said. "I am running away. I broke the window
in my room with a baseball and I know you will never forgive
me. So I am going to go be on my own now, from now on. I
packed a sweater and some potato chips so Mom, you know I'll
be fine. Do not try to come after me. By the time you read this,
I will already be gone. It's better this way. Good-bye forever.
Love, your son Dean." The group erupted in laughter. "He
came back by dinner, when he got hungry," Raymond added.
"We all pretended it had just never happened, and no one pun-
ished him for the broken window. We knew he cared too much
about family to be away too long." That was his message: Dean
cares about family. Dean will be a good husband. As the group
applauded, he took the letter, folded it back in its envelope, and
showed us the crayoned child's hand on the outside. "TO MY
PARENTS," it said. "OPEN RIGHT AWAY. IMPORTANT
STUFF." Then he brought it over and made a show of giving it
to Dean. The two men embraced. It was then I thought of my
own father's toast, somewhere upstairs in the house among his
stacks of papers maybe, his dark room empty as the wind blew
off the sea. *Such family happiness*, I thought, watching Raymond and Dean embrace that night. *I'm going to be a part of that
family, I'm in that embrace.*

Looking at Raymond lying on the ice in the fading winter light, his children standing above him, I thought of his reading of that letter of Dean's the night before our wedding. *Dear family, I am running away.* He was leaving. He had done something wrong, something capricious and beyond mending. *I know you will never forgive me. Do not try to come after me, for I will be gone.* He was running away. Far, far away. *It's better this way.* A child's escape. As far as the simple, bitter promise of freedom could carry him.

Part
Three

· XIII ·

In the Attic

SOON AFTER WE were first married, Dean and I moved to an apartment on the Upper West Side, where all the windows faced south. At night, we could watch as the lights came on in the apartment buildings down Broadway. If we held a mirror out the window, we could see the Hudson River reflected off to the west.

Evenings, I would listen to Dean play his guitar in the entryway of our apartment. The empty foyer, he said, was where we had the best acoustics. I would make dinner and he'd sit on a folding metal chair just outside the kitchen and sing; then the two of us would sit in the living room eating at the wooden table he had been given by his parents. It followed us from apartment to apartment, that table that had been the mainstay in the Jackson family kitchen for years. It was a beautiful, grown-up thing, I thought. If we were just playing house, living in a stage set that was our married life, then the wooden table, a deep chestnut, sturdy and gleaming, was the one true thing that grounded us center stage.

Dean wanted the simple life, and I wanted the most beautiful KitchenAid mixer we could afford. A pale teal color, I thought, or perhaps bright orange. Something also sturdy, grounded, grown-up, useful, but with color. This seemed a minor thing, but once we were married, we spent entire dazed sunlit Saturday afternoons walking into every hardware store on upper Broadway, and leaving empty-handed because we couldn't agree on a blender or a toaster, let alone a lifestyle. As the appliances broke down, one by one, over the course of five years, so did our marriage.

In truth, things had gotten somewhat confusing. Dean had been spending a lot of time floating in an isolation tank owned by an elderly couple on Central Park West with flowing white hair. I was an editor at a literary magazine, a job that often involved late nights taking writers out to dinner with my boss. My evenings and Dean's didn't blend all that well, at least not once he wanted me to get in the tank and I wanted him to accompany me to low-lit bistros all over town.

After five years, it felt as though all we had in common was the desire not to hurt each other's feelings. Late one Sunday morning, when I had the manuscript pages I was reading strewn all over our bed, the guitar music coming from the entryway stopped. Dean walked into the bedroom and said softly, "I don't know, it's like a house of cards and the cards are just, well, tumbling down." As he said it, his hands fluttered in the air and fell to his sides. I thought of dance class as a child, when the teacher would say, "Think of your hands as the leaves, girls, leaves in the autumn, tumbling to the ground." And I thought, *That's it. Dead leaves.*

After the leaf gesture, Dean took off his wedding ring and it lay in the palm of his hand, a little lost craft. We both looked at it, for a moment; then he shoved it deep in the pocket of his jeans. *Good-bye*, I thought. The gesture was so simple, brief, and yet final. He left a few weeks later, a duffle bag slung over one arm and a mountaineering pack on his back, like a kid catching the next bus back to college. The next day I called my mother in Paris. I told her about the whole thing. The tank and the KitchenAid mixer, the dead-leaf gesture and the ring. I told her about how I kept leaving paper clips from manuscripts in the bed by mistake. I told her about how the guitar music stopped one morning suddenly out of the blue. I told her that none of the things that were supposed to happen were going to happen anymore.

"I am completely undone by this," she told me over the phone. Then she added, "I am the only woman I *know* who isn't a grandmother." She paused, then put in, "I'm going to be in a wheelchair before one of the three of you gives me a grandchild."

To my unmarried sisters she confided, "Now I'm back to square one with you girls. Jesus Christ."

The next day, she called back and announced her arrival the following weekend. "I think I better come on," she said. "This is, after all, an emergency." I could hear the dramatic exhale, as if her cigarette smoke were drifting lazily through the phone wires, obscuring all my determined boundaries. It was brooding smoking. "You know I like to give you your space. Your 'space,' as you kids call it, but I've been brooding."

"Ma, I'm fine here," I said. "I'm doing just fine." But the

voice was not my own; it was a thin eggshell of a voice saying, "No, I mean yes, I mean no."

"I don't want my baby girl alone," she continued. "My tiny baby girl."

In truth, I was probably ready for her. In a dream I kept having, I was walking a street in New York. The streets were filled with men wearing gold wedding bands, men who kept coming up to me and telling me they never loved me. Then the bands disappeared. "But you don't even look like my husband," I told one of them.

In March in New York City, you can sometimes smell the dirt thaw. If it's an early spring, the streets give off a tang at once filthy and fresh, the sour along with the sweet promise of new bloom. The year Dean left, spring came early. My mother came soon after that.

"You know, I can't really help you with this," she warned as we drove down the LIE to the house. "If you had asked me a few years ago, well, I might have said a few things. But did anyone ask me?"

She appeared to be addressing herself in the small mirror of the sun visor, looking at her eyes in the mirror as she spoke. "I could have said a few long things back then," she repeated, telling the visor, "before it was too late. About marrying a boy like Dean. Who, let's face it, is a solid citizen in the world, handsome, polite, but is simply not yet grown-up. And yet. I quite liked him. John adored him." All this she told the sun visor. "But here we are. It's a mother's role, at a time like this, coming on."

In the years since my father had died, my mother had become something of a traveling road show. She lived in Paris much of the time, and took long cruises and safaris and stayed at châteaux and estates with people with impossibly exotic names and often with titles. She told me about it over the phone, lists and lists of foreign cities, elegant restaurants, all the new best friends she'd made god knows where, one more amusing than the last. Though she was alone now in the world, my mother liked to keep herself surrounded. And now she'd rolled the road show back into town, all the colored lights and clowns and jaunty music, the sideshow acts of bravery and daring, to my doorstep, for a few brief lessons in showmanship.

"Well, I'm here now," she declared. "Aren't I." Not a question. A statement of fact. An achievement.

She looked down and pulled a pile of glossy magazines from her carry bag and scattered them on her lap. "Here, dearie, get a load of this." She tapped a long red fingernail at a page of young women in poufy skirts. "Bubble skirts. Everyone in Paris is wearing them. I got one for each of you girls, to cheer you up." She sat back. Satisfied. She had brought back presents. "It's important to be chic. In times like this. To show the world you still know how to put yourself together. Baby girl." She patted my hand. "Look. A heart breaks sometimes. That's all there is to it. But you mark my words. We're going to get through this thing with grace and style and while we're at it with dignity, even if it kills us." She paused for a moment, watching silently as we drove along the LIE, passing a few exits. Then she spoke again. "The bottom line is, the show must go on. Trust your mother, that's all there is to that."

The morning that Dean left, I made him scrambled eggs, as if it were just another Saturday. I scrambled them with cheese and a dollop of mustard, which makes the eggs frothy. While I beat the mustard into the eggs, I thought, *All these years, I've never told him that I put mustard in the eggs. And now he'll never know why for the rest of his life his eggs are never again this frothy.* At that moment in the kitchen, beating eggs in a copper pot I held nestled in the crook of my arm, this was the biggest thought I'd had about the longevity of the rest of our lives, and that they would be lived separately. It was all I could manage. Eggs. Mustard. Froth. Kitchen tips.

When I returned home from work one night the following week, the blanket box in the foyer, where Dean sat to play his guitar, was gone. In its place, there was a note set on a folding chair.

"I know," it began, "it looks bare to me too. Give it a few weeks and if it still feels odd, I'll bring it back." There was some more talk of details: the car, forwarding mail, instructions about the fuse box in the back hall. Details of the quotidian. Then there was a lot of talk about paths and souls. How our souls had touched each other, but we were on different paths.

I lay on the floor in the empty foyer and looked up at the light fixture above me. It was a paper lantern we'd put over a bulb when we first moved in. The rest of the apartment was dark and quiet. Just one light above. No sound.

> *I bet birds talk like this, in the night sky, and we just don't understand them. "I love you, I love you, I love you. How come you never tell me that?" "I'm telling you now. I love you."*

It was very quiet in the foyer and nothing moved.

. . .

THE MORNING BY the sea, it rained. Heavy winds frothed the waves, the water steely as it crashed along the shoreline.

We were up in the attic. When I was a child, the attic was where my sisters and I would go in a storm. The reverberations up there were theatrical and spooky, and as children we loved being spooked, loved it the way one loves something loud, something forceful, something one can never control. The very drama of it put us in a world of our own: the rain falling in mad sparks of sound against the roof, the echo of the surf, thunder like a rip through the sky. It was a ghostly theater in the attic when it rained. One summer we had erected a shelter out of swaths of material, bright orange with white polka dots, in a series of swoops, which we thought reminiscent of Moroccan tents, pinning the bright cotton up with thumbtacks into the wooden beams along the eaves of the roof. It was our clubhouse, where we stored our collection of *Tiger Beat*, the teen fan magazine. We taped pictures of the Beatles, the Stones, and the Monkees on the walls of our orange tent. It was still there, the tent, the magazines, and the small portable record player that played our collection of 45s: "Mony Mony," "Hey Jude," "I'm a Believer."

Our mother had stored all the old childhood furniture under another eave in the attic, in preparation for grandchildren. In one corner was a high chair, white wood, with a pink elephant painted on the seat back. I reached out to touch it, and my finger made a long white line in the dust.

After Dean and I were married, all our wedding presents were stowed in the attic as we prepared for my father's funeral. With the occasion so quickly shifting modes, it seemed wrong to do otherwise. "We," the newlyweds, were suddenly "we," members of the family of the deceased, and our presents almost indecently irreverent. My mother had printed Tiffany cards for me to send out, saying I'd received their gift and would reply promptly. "That's what you do," she told me then, "so they don't think you forgot about them. Then you'll write later. Soon, mind you, but not now." Sympathy notes came in before I could send out any cards. And now the wedding presents waited. Blue Tiffany boxes, silver bags, colorful tissue paper, streamers and ribbons. We had never gone through them. So they remained where they'd been left, undisturbed, a huddled reminder of that weekend back in August 1983. Suddenly, unused and unopened, they were the only things between Dean and me to separate, and without my having to say it, my mother realized I couldn't do it alone.

She seated herself in an old orange beanbag chair that we'd had in the living room in the '60s. It was faded and collapsed, the Styrofoam balls flattened from use.

She blinked into the dim light at all the boxes, trunks, and discarded furniture. Cobwebs formed between the wood beams of the ceiling.

"Let's get this done before the weather clears," she said. She wriggled herself further into the beanbag. "Then we can take a nice walk on the beach."

The wind was howling. "Ma, it's dreadful out there."

"Oh," she said. "Trust your mother. It will clear. Your mother knows a few things."

The boxes were carefully marked. "TWO SALT AND PEP-PER SHAKERS, BRASS CANDLESTICKS, SOUP TU-REEN, CERAMIC COOKIE JAR (REALLY UGLY)," one box was labeled. "BRANDY SNIFTERS ($$$)," another said. I brought over a box marked "SILVER CHAFING DISH."

My mother eyed the boxes. "Jesus. I hope to god you wrote thank-you notes for all of this eventually," she said.

"Ma, it was five years ago."

"Your mother just wants to make sure. There's some pretty good loot here, it looks like."

She looked out over the presents. "Those Tiffany note cards I gave you to send out were not to take the place of actual thank-you notes, let me remind you."

In fact, I never sent out the Tiffany note cards she had given me. Instead of thank-you notes going out, condolence notes came pouring in. "It was a beautiful wedding," read one. "I am so sorry for your loss."

"People remember these things, dearie," my mother said. "The rule is, you have one year to write a thank-you note for a wedding present. Not a day more. So it's important. I told you that umpteen times."

"Ma, don't stew."

"Your mother is just checking," she said, "is all."

"Okay, you checked." I held up the silver chafing dish. "What the hell is a chafing dish, anyway? How'd it get that name?"

"*That* one happens to be very expensive. Who gave you that?"

"I don't remember."

"It's very good sterling silver." She took off the ornate top and held it up. I could see her red lips reflected in the shine. "Take it home. It came from our side of the family."

"How can you be sure."

"Peh, c'mon. It's shows real taste." She wrote it on the list on the column under my name. "Let's give him things he can really use. That life preserver, for example. Who gave you a life preserver?"

"It goes with the canoe."

The canoe, our beautiful pea green boat, had spent the past five years accumulating dust in my mother's garage.

"A canoe. Who gives such presents?" my mother asked. "A canoe in New York City. What the hell were you planning to do with it?"

"I don't know. Circumnavigate the island? Hang it out the window on upper Broadway and use it as a planter with a row of geraniums?"

"Please," my mother said, shaking her head. "Don't get me started." She added the life preserver and the canoe to the column on Dean's side of the list. "Bring on the next item," she said, waving her pen in the air.

The next box was china dinner plates. A dozen of them, pearly gray, almost pinkish, opaque, with the luster of the inside of a conch shell. I remembered picking them out. I remembered standing in the store, afraid to touch one, as if it would slip through my fingers, shatter right there, and everyone would know the marriage was a joke. A facade. That we were not ready for adult things like marriage and fine china.

"You never used these? You never thought to come and get them?"

"We never had cause to."

"You eat. God knows he ate."

"I don't know. It was safer to use the old stuff."

She held up her pen. "Look. China breaks sometimes. You have to be careful, but it doesn't mean you don't use it."

*Look, a heart breaks sometimes. You have to be careful, but
    it doesn't mean you don't use it.
Patch as much as you need; it doesn't hurt.*

"I don't know, I guess I was scared," I admitted.

She laughed. "You little thing? What do you have to be so
afraid of?"

She went on. "Let him have the goddamn china then." She
wrote down, "TIFFANY DINNER PLATES, ONE DOZEN."
"Fine, done. Done and done. Life goes on. You don't dwell, dearie. You don't wallow and brood."

I closed the box. *Good-bye*, I was thinking. They looked so
serene, lying there. I'd lost them, and they didn't even break.
Something more inept than just slipping through fingers. Or
maybe just that inept. Just that dumb and tragic.

I thought then of my father's note on the envelope of the
last Franklin story he gave me: "*JJ dear, here is an installment of
Franklin. I finally managed it.*

"*You're getting too old for my stories, but as you keep asking for
them, your wish is my command. But this is the last one I believe.
With love and pride, Daddy.*"

That was how he left us: "*This is the last one I believe.*"

"Look, you don't want these things sitting around haunting
you forever, trust me. Sometimes," my mother said, making
points with the pen on her pad for emphasis, "you just have to
accept that you lose things. They go. That doesn't mean you
don't use them."

Loss. After the episode of the man who drowned in front
of our eyes when I was a child, I had come to imagine "loss"

as a stuff, a substance that I could hold in my hand. It would be the grainy consistency of sand or cremated ashes, and if someone came along and offered me more I would say, "Loss? Thanks. No. I don't need any more. I've got all I can ever use right here." As if to prove it, I'd hold out my hand. I thought that might protect me from more loss on the perilous dune, a handful of grain in the palm of my hand.

She drew a double line at the bottom of the list. Then she looked up. "You know," she said, "I wish I could have been a better mother to you then, at the wedding. But I was just . . . numb."

I felt I needed to say something to reassure her then. She was a mother after all. Only a mother. Nothing superhuman. "I know, Ma, we all were. Numb. We were zombies. I was the zombie bride of the apocalypse."

She smiled then. "Tee," she said. "Dearie, you do amuse me. You make your mother laugh."

I thought then of what the minister had told me the morning of my wedding: "You're laughing, but I know you don't think this is funny." The joke reflex was my family's way of glossing over things. Our way of trying not to feel. I didn't know at the time that it was dangerous to gloss over things, to not speak up, to try not to feel. At the time, it felt safe.

> *We're going to get through this thing with grace and style*
> *even if it kills us.*
> *I wish I could have been a better mother to you then, but I was*
> *numb.*

In one quiet corner of the attic, a series of large wardrobe boxes huddled under the slanted wooden beams. The name of a local moving company, Home Sweet Home, was stamped in black lettering on each tall dusty box. One box was labeled, "MRS. MCCULLOCH: FORMALWEAR 1960–1975." Inside, her feathered ball gowns were encased in thick plastic bags, the feathers flat, matted down over the years. The boxes smelled of mothballs.

"Whew, Ma, look at this," I said. "Your dresses." Things forgotten came back. The black velvet with white ostrich around the neck was her favorite. Another was navy blue organdy with dyed-blue feathers ringed at the wrists like muffs.

In another box was her Lilly Pulitzer collection.

When we were young, all the summer mothers used to stand at the rail station on Friday evening waiting for the train from Penn Station, the weekly Cannonball, as it was called, to deliver the fathers from the city. I remember the mothers in their brightly colored flowery shifts, hair frosted silvery in the manner of the model Jean Shrimpton and freshly done in neat arrangements behind matching headbands. The mothers wore pastel sandals, pale pink frosted Slicker lipstick, and gold earrings. Though my sisters and I had no father working in the city during the week, sometimes we would go along with friends—it was always a special occasion. We'd lay pennies on the track long before arrival, when the first whistle blew in the distance to the left, announcing the train had just left the station at the Water Mill stop and was heading our way. Then, when the train rushed by, all the fathers would wave from the windows. Children on the platform would jump up and down and laugh; the mothers in their Lillys would talk to one another, and as they spotted each other's husbands, they would point them out: "Molly, there's Jerry, looks like he got a haircut during the week." "Janet, Henry's right there." "Jake is on the last car, Mary, the caboose, see, there he is, honey." When the train came to a stop, the fathers would amble off in an even file, jumping down the last few steps onto the platform, hair mussed, in shirtsleeves, ties off and collars unbuttoned, carrying jackets and briefcases in their hands. Spotting their families, the fathers would open their arms, mouths in broad smiles, ready to be enveloped in the hugs of their clan. After the train passed, my sisters and I would make our way back down to the tracks to collect the flattened pennies, while the children whose fathers had been delivered to them stood on the platform, wrapped in grateful embraces, before heading out to the parking lot filled with wood-sided station wagons.

Our own father would never appear among the fathers on the train. He was at this point in the late afternoon well into his first evening scotch. We would return home those Fridays, dropped off by one or another of the train families, the father instead of the mother now driving the station wagon. Already, the kids in the car would be yelling the week's news at their father: "Jerry got thrown in the pool!" "Izzie got first in the freestyle meet!" "The boys on the soccer team peed on the raspberry bushes!" "Can we go fishing with you tomorrow pleeze, and can I bait the hooks all by myself?" "There are fireworks on Main Beach Saturday night! Mom said we can go with a picnic dinner, 'kay, Dad?" The silence of our house as we entered the foyer had a gray, haunting weight to it after the festive clamor of the train station children and the weekly return of their heroic fathers.

These fathers appeared in the winter too. In New York City blizzards, doormen with snow piled an inch high on the flats of their caps blew their whistles along Park Avenue into the hush of the storm, to hail the few lone cabs out in the weather. The cabs plodded through the thick snow making tracks, the glow of their lights visible from far off in the white mist. They pushed with effort down the wide avenue, wipers clearing the fat fresh flakes off the windshields as they progressed closer in the storm. Along Park Avenue, fathers, the same fathers, now on cross-country skis, parkas over their gray suits, in wool beanies and ski goggles, their briefcases strapped to their backs, glided down Park Avenue toward the gray Pan Am building dividing uptown from downtown. Their skis made long tracks as they followed each other, silent in the newly fallen snow, on their way to gleaming offices in Midtown Manhattan. These same heroic fathers who rode the Cannonball express train out to East Hampton on the Friday afternoons of summer; now in their winter garb braved the elements. Upstairs, in the quiet of our apartment, my father in his pajamas and bathrobe sat with his books in the living room, a cup of tea, a boiled egg, and a can of Budweiser on a folding table by his side.

"Try one of the dresses on," my mother said. "One of the feathers. It would look so cute on you."

I looked at the dresses in their plastic wrap and imagined the feel. The stiff bodices, too big for my frame, the feathers tickling my nose, getting in my mouth, the smell of mothballs and faint perfume.

"No," I said. "I don't think I want to, Ma."

"Or a Lilly then. Lillys never go out of style, dearie. Take it from me. You could pull it off. Add a little color to that black you wear all the time. We could get them taken in for you in a

snap. Don't you want a dress of mine for your own? It would
be fun for you to have."

"Maybe," I said. I pushed the box aside and pulled out another from behind. It was labeled, "MRS. MCCULLOCH
DRESSES, 1950s ON."

I pulled out a dress from the box. It was soft silk, cheong-
sam, royal blue, with a high collar, cap sleeves, small pearl buttons down one side, and a slit up the leg on the other. It felt
elegant and graceful as I held it in my hands. "This is what I'd
like to try on."

She reached out an arm from the beanbag. "Let's see," she
said. "Give it to me."

She held the dress up in both hands, taking off her reading
glasses to get a better look, and thought quietly for a moment.
Then she smiled and put the dress in her lap. It lay there on top
of the legal pad listing wedding presents. "No," she said. "Dearie, this is mine. Daddy brought it back to me from his travels
to the Far East, back when we were just courting."

"It's so lovely, though," I said. I imagined the silk gently
brushing my bare feet as I buttoned it up, my hair swept high
up on my head as I wore it out. "I think it would fit me. Or we
could maybe just take this one in."

With one hand, she pinched the fabric lightly and rubbed it
between her fingers. "No, no, I don't think so."

"Ma, you will never wear this dress again. You didn't even
know it was up here. It would never even fit."

"Look, you're getting my emeralds when I go. So don't push
it." She looked down at the dress pooled in her lap, the soft silk
luminous.

"You're young yet," she told me. "Someday, you'll have a

lovely dress like this of your own. Maybe even someday if you're lucky someone will give you one as a special present, some nice man. As for me," she went on, "this is all I have left."

I think I'm lonely. One letter changed, and I would be lovely. What would that be like?

"Dearie, your father wasn't perfect. No man is. But when he came along, he changed my whole life. We had some happy, happy times."

My mother had had her portrait painted in that very same silk dress when she was a young bride. In the portrait, she sits by an open window. Beyond her is a small balcony, iron balustrade, and beyond that the cityscape. Rooftops, buildings so far away the windows are but dots of gray in the painter's palette. Her black hair is cut short in bangs along her brow, flipped in curls just at her chin. This was the look she had in all the photos of her courtship with my father, and in the photos of her life as a young mother. Almond eyes, clear white skin, her face composed. Her mouth was a ruby red in the portrait. It hung in our living room for years. In a black-and-white photo taken years later, she sits in a curved leopard-print loveseat under the portrait. The face is the same, but her gaze is steely, her mouth set firm. It must have been the mid-'70s when the second picture was taken. Her hair is still black, but with a white streak coming up from her hairline, sprayed and brushed back off her face. She wears tartan slacks and a pale turtleneck sweater, patent leather pumps with gold buckles on the toe, as was her style at the time. In the twenty years between those images, the hope and openness of the first gave way to the hardened resolve of the second. On her leopard loveseat, she braced herself.

"Life was not easy with your father," she said. "You know that. Marriage never is, or we wouldn't be sitting here in this mess, with all these boxes of unopened wedding presents and boxes of old clothes and old baby furniture no one has ever used." On the beanbag chair, she seemed so small. "Yet."

Stories of my mother's young life emerged rarely. When she would tell us about it, she would be angry. "No one loved me," she would say, or "Everyone liked Sissy best." Declarations, not anecdotes. When I imagined her young life, I pictured her in a house with strangers, alone. This would be followed with a softer voice: "When your father came along, he changed my whole life."

The morning tapered into afternoon as we sat in the attic. "Help your old ma up," she said when we were done, putting out an arm from the depths of the beanbag chair.

As we reached the bottom of the attic stairs, a blast of light shone down the hall from the window. "Look," she said. She tapped a ruby fingernail against the pane.

"See, what did I tell you? I wasn't crazy. No more rain."

The waves broke in graceful furls of foam, pushing in even lines toward the shore.

"Look," she told me then. "A mother can fix a lot of things, but she cannot fix a broken heart. Not even I can do that. But I can tell you this, little one. You'll never carry a weight too heavy to bear. You're too strong for that. Okay? The rest of it takes time. Hearts don't heal overnight. I wish it didn't take so long, but it does. That's just the way it goes."

Look, china breaks, that doesn't mean you don't use it.
Look, a heart breaks, that doesn't mean you don't use it.
Patch as much as you need; it doesn't hurt.

She took my hand in hers and squeezed four times. It was an old game. *Do. You. Love. Me.*

I squeezed back three times. *Yes. I. Do.*

She squeezed twice. *How. Much.*

I gave her one big squeeze, to say, *To smithereens and back.* Then I squeezed hers four times, she followed with three, then I with two, and finally she took my hand in both of hers and squeezed as hard as she could. We laughed. "Ouch," I said. I shook my hand. "Ma!"

Together we stood side by side at the window and watched the waves break toward the shore in even curls of foam. The glinting sunlight made crazy diamonds across the water.

"Look," she said then. "At the end of the day, that's what we do. We march on. We don't dwell. If I've done my job right, that's what I've taught you. There's always tomorrow. Right?"

For a time, I didn't answer. She squeezed my hand again and repeated, "Am I right?"

"Okay, of course. Right."

"Right?"

"Yes, right."

"Baby girl, trust your old ma," she said. "It's going to be a perfectly glorious day."

· XIV ·

The House

"THE HOUSES ARE all gone under the sea," T. S. Eliot wrote in one of the songs in *Four Quartets*. I thought of that line as we packed up the house on the last summer we owned it, and of another of Eliot's, from *The Waste Land*: "These fragments I have shored against my ruins."

Beyond the sweet, gentle smell of the tangle of wild honeysuckle in the driveway, the high two-toned trill of the morning bobwhite, the cold watermelon seed shooting down a shirt, gleefully spit by a boy cousin all the girls in town admired, beyond all this inevitably there were the darker memories. Of hearing about my father leaving the house for the last time on an ambulance stretcher. Of my mother, living on for twenty years in a grief that became a rage, her final summers spent in the house by the sea in a wheelchair, accompanied by a nurse, by occasional family and friends she no longer recognized but reflexively cursed. By the endless beat of the waves that just keep coming and coming.

My mother lived on for twenty years after my father died, and fifteen years after the death of her sister, my aunt Jeanne. Determined not to be one of the army of women, she, soon after my aunt was gone, captured the attention of a handsome widower called Harry ("His poor wife's deathbed wasn't even cold yet when your mother swooped in," her friends all clucked admiringly), and Harry took up residence on my father's side of the couch. He and my mother smoked and talked together for the years they had left. When she was paralyzed from the waist down with neuropathy and I was remarried and had my first child, Sam, Harry would wheel my mother alongside me as I wheeled Sam in his stroller. Ever flirtatious, she'd wave at Sam and giggle, and he'd coo and gurgle back, and I know that scene made her happier than probably anything else.

"You girls are so slow to get married and have children, I'll be in a wheelchair before I have any grandchildren," she used to say, and about that, like other things, she ended up being right. After Harry died from a rapidly growing form of cancer one year, my mother, paralyzed, on dialysis, and demented, despite her wishes to not ever be without her grace, style, or dignity, nevertheless lived on.

Often late at night in those years she would call me, demanding I get on a plane to Paris, where our father had "run off with a tootsie," or that I go to jail and bail Harry out. She called me Sissy, and I knew she was already talking with the dead. It was Sissy, fifteen years gone at this point, who she was entreating to sort out the messes her men had gotten themselves into, these men who even in her dementia she saw as having abandoned her.

For the living, she had nothing but increasing rage.

In the end, my mother was in a hospital bed in Mount Sinai in New York City. Her housekeeper, per her instructions, came by every day and did her makeup and put on her earrings and did her hair.

We're going to get through this thing with grace and style
   even if it kills us.

Her kidneys had failed, and one of her legs had become gangrenous and would have to be amputated if she was to have a shot at surviving. I thought of what she had said to my father all those years before: "You didn't want us to do anything heroic to save you if you no longer had your dignity. Remember, that was the promise we made. . . "

Yet I realized too, as the executor of her living will, that in signing the DNR order I would with a pen be putting an end to her life. That pen in my hand felt weaponized, wrong, too powerful. At the doctor's urging, I reread the instructions she had left to us, and I realized how truly hard it must have been for her to put an end to my father's life even when there was no hope of recovery. *We've given up hope. Where has hope gone?* The power to end someone's life should not be this easy, I thought, a scratch of a pen on paper. Or maybe it should be. Maybe it's just that simple.

My sister Darcy and I convened her best friends, Nancy and Mu, to come visit and help us out with the decision. The same two women apparently responsible for our lives, in talking our mother into marrying our father, were now going to be indispensable in deciding her death. At this point, both were widows. Al the lawyer had died, and Nancy's fifth husband had died as well. Yet Mu was still elegant, wrapped in a purple cloak, and Nancy was still scrappy and no-nonsense.

"You have to let her go," Nancy told us. We were standing in the lobby of Mount Sinai Hospital. Above us, our mother lay in the geriatric wing. "Right, Mu?"

"Honey," said Mu to me, because Mu always called everyone honey, "it's time."

"We're not getting any younger," Nancy added. Nancy's eyes were going, and she wore thick lenses that made her eyes enormous as she looked at me. "She wouldn't want this. That's all you have to keep in mind." She folded her arms over her chest and shifted her weight to one hip. "None of us would."

They were not mournful; instead they were determined and direct. *None of us would.* The "three little maids from school." They had seen one another through their adult lives, husbands, children, and now they would see to one another's deaths.

Mu put her hand lightly on Nancy's arm. Mu's hand was flecked with age spots, her veins bulged, but her fingers were long and graceful, the deep sapphire ring Al gave her still on her hand. "Nance, let me drop you in a cab, honey," she said. To them, there was no more discussion. They were leaving.

"You girls know the right thing to do," Nancy said as they locked arms and walked together across the hospital lobby toward the revolving glass doors. We watched them get into a cab, the hospital doorman lowering first Nancy and then Mu into the back seat, and we watched as they drove off down Fifth Avenue, the taillights of their taxi retreating into the distance as they made their way into the evening.

Back upstairs, I took the living will out of my pocket, and at the nurse's desk I signed my name.

At the time, I had been filling out applications to preschool for my daughter, Charlotte, and under "relationship" on the DNR form I reflexively wrote "mother" on the line below my signature. As I corrected it and wrote "daughter," I realized that I was writing it for the very last time.

We waited for my sister Catherine to arrive, and then the plan was to take our mother home to hospice care, though she didn't make it that long. As soon as Catherine arrived, our mother was gone. And so when my sister Darcy and I arrived at the hospital, she lay there, still with her earrings on and her hair coiffed, Catherine beside her in the chair. At the funeral home, the three of us identified the body and I stood a long time over the casket, a simple pine box, looking at the peace I found in her face. In many years, I had not seen her this peaceful. She was beautiful in her serenity, a beauty that erased the lines from scowls and grimaces. At last she was at peace.

"Excuse me, may I ask an irrelevant question," I asked the funeral director. We sat in his office, leafing through pages of his urn catalogue. The large book was bound in leather, splayed out across his desk. Just to his right, above the door frame, an orange "No Exit" sign was posted. "Do people tease you for sitting under a 'No Exit' sign?" I asked him. "I mean, isn't that the idea here, the ultimate 'No Exit,' so to speak?"

He looked up and said, "I see you like the turquoise blue urn. It costs extra because it's unique, but it's well worth it."

"We really should get the turquoise urn," Catherine said. "We have to. It's the color of her favorite muumuu."

"Okay, no exit, I get it," my sister Darcy said to me. "*Huis Clos.*" She nodded. "The one time Sartre is funny."

"We're taking her to Switzerland," Catherine told the man.

"She will love it there," he said, somewhat nonsensically. "She'll be in our crematorium in the Bronx waiting for you whenever you ladies are ready to fly her there."

This added a sense of new urgency for Catherine, who said, "She won't like waiting around in the Bronx. Not for one minute."

Of the three of us, Catherine seemed to be able to most closely channel our mother. She had also quite naturally developed her knack for making use of a broad palette of accents. So, with a British one that would have made our mother proud, she said to the undertaker, "Lovely then," and lightly clapped her hands. "Please would you kindly arrange for everything, and we'll be on our way."

We took our mother to join our father in Lake Lugano in her turquoise urn. It was just the three of us this time, no half siblings, though my sisters brought their husbands. As the motorboat rocked in the middle of Lake Lugano, and the cowbells rang in the distance, one of my brothers-in-law struggled to get the canister of ashes opened. On the boat's radio, "Spanish Dancer" played at soft volume:

> *Oh mama when you were a young girl*
> *Did you ever love a man so much*

The woman driving the boat spoke to us in Italian. She pointed at all three of us and said, "*Tre sorelle?*"

We nodded. "Yes, three sisters."

"I can tell," she said in English. "You have the same laugh."

We put our mother's ashes in the lake to join our father's.

The two of them are one, I thought as the water lapped against the boat in the flat calm. *Dancing together as one.*

"We live on such a perilous dune," my mother would say as the August storm season approached and the waves bounded up to our dune. "All of this could just go"—and she'd snap her fingers—"like that."

The house by the sea ended up being on a perilous dune indeed, though in retrospect I realized that my mother had been speaking less about weather than about the vicissitudes of inherited property. As was the case with many houses founded on the notion of family legacy in the nineteenth and twentieth centuries, economics and other exigencies conspired so that after my mother died, the house by the sea fell to us to sell, and thus my father's dream of a family compound was washed away—not by any ministrations of nature, unless one thinks of the IRS as a natural disaster. As fate would have it, the *L* fell off the driveway sign the year she died, and Children at Play became what it suddenly was: Children at Pay.

Perhaps my father should have realized you can't sink roots in sand. Only my mother, raised in hurricanes, foresaw the perilous *"après moi, le déluge"* truth.

After casting about for someone to carry out the sale, my sisters and I hired an icily handsome real estate broker named Ed whose chiseled good looks and slick bravado put one in mind of the superhero the Silver Surfer. He slapped a price tag on our beloved house befitting, he told us, its status in the minds of the "hedgies" now purchasing the real estate in town.

"The whatsies?"

He didn't look up from the papers he was leafing through.

"Hedge fund managers, hedgies. The hedgies and celebs are lapping up houses like this." He snapped his fingers. "Primo real estate," Ed told us. "It rocks their cashmere socks."

"Faded glory, a vestige of a world gone by," Ed wrote as a description on the tear sheet, next to the pictures of our house taken both from the land and from the air.

"Now, some," Ed the broker warned us, "might call your place a 'tear-down'—so don't be alarmed if they do."

"Our mother would die," Catherine said. "It would kill her."

"She is dead, honey," Ed said with a voice so gentle it was as though he were breaking the news to us for the first time. "I'm sorry." Then he shifted back to broker-speak. "I just want to prepare you ladies." He looked up. "Uncle Ed cares about you. That's no joke. So"—he took a deep breath—"I suggest you all take your kids and go down to the beach. Stay out of earshot of what you don't need to hear. I know it can be hard to sell a home, but really, trust me, people flip real estate all the time." He shook his head. "Selling a childhood home can be rough, so take the kids and go make a day of it, relax. On the beach. With those striped umbrellas in the back of my van, why not. I'll bring them out. And while you're down there you might throw a ball or a Frisbee around. Do you have cute dogs, any of you? You know, suggest how it can be for a family here." He snapped his fingers again. "Mood setting."

People flip real estate all the time. In my mind, I saw a home being placed on one side of a child's seesaw; then the owner would run and leap on the other side. The home would jump in the air, do a flip, and land upright on the ground, suddenly simply a house, a property—free of any deep association with home. It seemed to me a disingenuous term, meant to make it look like child's play when in fact it was never easy. Home base, homeward bound, give me a home, it was not child's play to leave one's home, and the equation between home and real estate became a blurred line. Where, in this equation, do we fit the delicate calculus of memory?

At that point, on the South Fork of Long Island, new residents were also landing their private planes at our local airport, and our house was right on the flight path from New York City. We gamely suggested to Ed that to court his target group of buyers, arriving each weekend not by the Cannonball but by private plane, we might send a young nephew or two up a ladder to write "4 SALE" in white paint all along the roof of Children at Play.

Ed laughed, a short snort of a laugh, until he stopped, mid-laugh, and said, "Cute." Then he went back to the notes he had on a clipboard. "Did anyone get married here?" he asked. "Maybe we could have some pictures in the house, along the mantelpiece in the living room, of celebration and happy times. Could really work as a sales pitch, particularly for the young fiancées and wives coming through."

I thought of Nonnie's collection of table settings. *A table setting lasts forever.*

"We have no pictures," I answered.

"Then," he said, "we'll have to go with the kids. Do they play on that swing set?" He pointed to the garden where Dean and I had gotten married years before, and where more recently my mother had had her gardener erect a colorful play area for her young grandchildren. "If they do, or even if they don't, can they do so when I bring couples by for a second visit? That way, they see beach and kids, dogs, toys, visit number one, then visit two, swing set. Ladies, sounds like we have a plan. Okay, let's get to work." And he made several notes on the clipboard. "I like it," he said, writing. "Slam dunk."

We buffed the house, made each bed so not a wrinkle showed, swept the long halls clean of sand from toddler feet, and when potential buyers came, we removed our entire menagerie from the premises down to the beach, where they could look cute and inspirational to young couples coming by to do exactly what our father had done in 1964: put down roots. Only now it appeared the putting down of roots also came with the desire to make a statement.

As we waited on the beach, Ed welcomed intruders who sniffed and prodded, pulling open closet doors and inspecting views from all possible vantage points. The private jets crossed overhead each Friday, traveling east from New York City to the East Hampton Airport.

"I still liked our marketing scheme best," I told my sisters one day on the beach, pointing up at one of the small jets flying overhead while our children dug in the sand to make forts and moats. "These people right there might well bid on the house if they saw our '4 SALE' sign on the roof."

One day, gazing up, we saw Howard Stern, the "shock jock" radio personality, poised above my mother's prized geraniums on the deck outside her bedroom. The implausible image, his black shirt, black aviator glasses, and signature black tresses amid the gentle arrangement of pink flowers just beyond her boudoir, would have so mortified my mother and endlessly amused my father that I couldn't help but appreciate it as a ridiculous reminder of the difference between home and real estate.

. . .

The final summer, as we were packing up, we went looking for my mother's ball gowns in the attic. It was late one night, and braced by the spirit of nostalgia and wine, my sisters and I trudged the boxes down two flights of stairs to the living room and started pulling them out. There was the burgundy one with the dyed-black ostrich-feather cuffs, the emerald green with the fitted bodice and long train. What resulted from the sudden discovery was a spontaneous fashion show for our husbands, each of us taking turns doing exaggerated catwalk steps around the couches, littering feathers along the pale green carpet in our wake. In a video taken that night, the men are smoking cigars, while my sisters and I, flushed and giddy, segue from one costume change to the next. Yet the mirth had a disdain to it that was at once murky and palpable, that such a costume would have been so much a part of the accepted pattern of our life, and that that life—the sheen, the glow, the mythic glamour—could pass from our hands so easily and definitively, and all we could do was watch.

But what was it, really, that was passing? In truth, wearing a feathered ball gown, I discovered that night, is an uncomfortable sensation. The gown hangs heavily on the shoulders and makes a discordant swish as you labor the fabric across the room. Furthermore, the feathers tickle the cheeks. Simply putting on my mother's costume, smelling, vaguely, the stale whisper of her Chanel perfume, I calculated that this outfit, plus the teetering on high heels for an entire evening, could not have been as glamorous or regal as it was painful and tedious. On some of the white feathers, there were faint stains of her bright red lipstick. My mother always wore very, very red lipstick.

By the end of the night, the entire collection of dresses lay abandoned, collapsed like overspent party girls in a pile on the couch. Just then I thought of my wedding dress all those years before, how it lazed on the chair in the hotel room the morning after I married Dean; rumpled, sand at the hem, a costume of fragile lace I put on to carry through with grace and style, no matter what the circumstance. Now here were my mother's long-ago dresses, also collapsed like worn-out party girls. We drank one more toast to the passing of time, and in the end, I think my cousin's daughters, both girls in their early twenties, took a few back to college with them—good for a party maybe, get a laugh, one of them said, shrugging.

"This was an amazing place to be a kid," I said to my sisters the last afternoon, looking out over the sea as the movers packed up the last of the living room, wrapping the little cabbage-leaf and romaine-leaf cigarette lighter holders in newspaper, carrying out my father's black leather armchair and my parents' couch to their waiting trucks. The couch our parents shared when they no longer shared much of anything else.

Amaze: to fill with wonder. Also: to bewilder.

Three little girls in matching dresses following their parents through a life they could no more accurately explain than apologize for. Down by the wild tangle of honeysuckle off the guest cottage, I pulled the old driveway sign out of the dirt that afternoon and placed it in the back of my van for safekeeping. "Children at P_ay."

The summer before we sold the house, I had taken my young children, Sam and Charlotte, to Georgica Beach so they could boogie-board under a lifeguard's gaze. It was a late August day, the water warm, the sky dark blue in anticipation of autumn. The corn was lush and tall in every field we passed as we headed toward the parking lot. For a while Sam and Charlotte flung themselves through the surf, buoyant puppies. When they were exhausted, they dragged their boards out, and the three of us stood together at the shore looking out at the view I had watched my whole life up to that point from the quilted bedroom at the top of the stairs in the house by the sea. The waves that just keep coming and coming and coming. Sam stared quietly for a while at the horizon while he caught his breath; then he turned to me with his gap-toothed smile, his eyes full of the sheer exuberance of wonder, and said, "Think about it, Mom. Infinity. Come on. I mean, you gotta love it." Being almost nine at the time, Sam liked to boggle his brain with big concepts like that. And I thought, *So there it is. His and Charlotte's legacy isn't about any cushion of wealth that's going to soften their ride. Their legacy is infinity, the sense of infinite possibility. Possibilities are endless, after all, endless as the waves. They just keep coming and coming and coming.*

Soon after my mother died, I went to see Helen. She was living in a small apartment alone down the road from their family house. After Raymond left, she had had a brief career as a Representative in the Maine state legislature, and I loved that after years of nurturing her family, she was busy nurturing the entire township. She had cartons of small Maine blueberries in a basket she gave me to take home. "For your kids," she said. "A little taste of Maine. I remember you love them, honey." And once we'd settled into her living room, she told me this:

"You know, one of my regrets is that I wasn't stronger in standing up to your mother, the weekend of your wedding to

Dean. It was wrong that we stayed, that we went ahead with the wedding with your father in a coma, and I knew it at the time. All I wanted to do was throw my family back in the car and drive home to Maine. We didn't belong there. You kids were too young to make that call, but I should have. I wish I could have been a stronger mother to you two, but your own mother was so imperious, I was cowed. I didn't dare."

I wish I could have been a stronger mother, but I didn't dare.
I wish I could have been a better mother to you then, but I was
    numb.

One day shortly before that visit to Helen, my daughter, Charlotte, had come home from school and told me she was going to die. "Gus told me I didn't have a heart." Her almond eyes, the same eyes as my mother's, grew wide. "And if I don't have a heart, I'm going to die."

"I think, maybe, Gus meant that you aren't returning his affection. Not that you're going to die."

Look, a heart breaks, that doesn't mean you don't use it.
If I don't have a heart, I'm going to die.

"So then I'm not going to die."

"No. Trust your mother, you're not going to die."

"Phew," she said.

We were heading toward Hudson River Park, Charlotte beside me on her scooter. To steer she dragged the toe of her blue high-top sneaker along the cobblestones outside our house. Once we were safely to the other side of the treacherous cross-

ing at the West Side Highway, Charlotte tore down the promenade south along the Hudson, off to meet her friend Gus at
the pier. Gus, who earlier in the day she had disdained, now
was once again her main man. She darted confidently through
the oncoming traffic of baby strollers, couples hand in hand,
dogs without leashes. Under her helmet, her penny-colored
hair flew up behind. "Careful!" I wanted to yell. "Come back!"
But Charlotte was already well beyond earshot, riding high and
free. Someday, I was thinking, no amount of knee pads and
helmets I could provide would protect her from having her own
heart broken. I knew that, but I also knew I'd never stop trying.

> *A mother can fix a lot of things, but she cannot fix a broken
>   heart.*
> *Look, a heart breaks, that doesn't mean you don't use it.*
> *Patch as much as you need; it doesn't hurt.*
> *Trust your mother, you're not going to die.*

The last time I saw our house, I didn't intend to find it there. I
wasn't looking for its presence, but rather its absence. The new
owners, a young couple with plans to start a family, tried to put
in the very amenity my mother had scoffed at, air-conditioning,
and the shambling old infrastructure couldn't sustain it. My sister Darcy had heard at a holiday party that the house had been
knocked down. And so, visiting the area later that week, on
New Year's Eve, I left my own family, Sam and Charlotte and
their father, in the car down at the end of the driveway by the
honeysuckle bush, and walked alone to see the barren site. But
the news had been wrong, or slightly wrong. The house was
indeed slated for demolition, but it had only been demolished

on the inside. The windows were blown out, in some places the frames charred black. So it had been a tear-down after all.

Soon it would be gone, and in its stead a brand-new state-of-the-art facsimile would be erected, with all the modern conveniences: air-conditioning, a pool, a gated security system. The tangle of wild honeysuckle would be cut down, and the security gate at the driveway would be braced by two stone pillars, the street address engraved on a bronze plaque at the entry.

The salty air smelled faintly of wood smoke, a winter fire burning in the hearth of a living room nearby. In my childhood, summer nights often smelled like this as the sparks of numerous bonfires up and down the shore lit up the beachfront. On the Fourth of July, fireworks launched from the Main Beach nearby burst just beyond us, as if we could reach out and touch them. The resultant booms made the house tremble while shrieks of children's laughter pierced the air. We squatted by the fire with long sticks melting marshmallows for s'mores, our sunburned faces and sweatshirts lightly illuminated in the glow. We ran relay races along the soft sand later in the season while all the fathers, and later our husbands, stood at the water's edge with fishing rods surf-casting, hoping to bring in the blues and stripers that ran just offshore at sundown, as the mothers tended littler kids in a circle around the fire.

Maybe I conjured it, that winter day, the warm smell of wood smoke on the deserted beach, or the smell wafted up from the charred driftwood scattered here and there from bonfires last season. Under demolition our house looked hurt to me, blistered by circumstance. And yet at the same time noble, serene, and resolute.

The fading light glowed in long rays across the beachfront

as I turned to retrace my steps up along the dunes to my car and my waiting family. It was almost dusk. The magic hour. Or, as the French would say, "*l'heure bleue.*" The hour when anything might happen. I took one last look back. In the few fragments of broken glass still clinging to the sills of the windows of the house, the last light of the day reflected red. When I was young, and the windows were enflamed by the setting sun, it appeared to my naively intoxicated imagination as if the house were filled to the brim with roses. As my mother would have had it, tomorrow would be a perfectly glorious day.

Acknowledgments

SPECIAL THANKS ARE due first and foremost to JDT, for his generous insight, his gentle grace, and his undying support, all of which completely inform this story.

This book would never have happened without the wonder that is Karen Rinaldi. She signed this project when it was a three-thousand-word essay, then she waited me out while I thrashed and dithered; she continued to believe in me, and in this project, beyond all reasonable doubt. Every single day she sets a kickass example as a skilled and dedicated editor, as a passionate and honest writer, as an exemplary mother, a loyal friend, and as one of the bravest women I know. My agent Binky Urban similarly waited me out, and even when I felt I had to dive behind a couch to hide when I'd run into her, being simply out of excuses for why this book wasn't done, knowing she was there believing in me was a gift and a miracle. Thanks to the Harper Wave team, Hannah Robinson, Penny Makras, and ace publicity director Yelena Gitlin Nesbit. These women answered my every question and awed me on a regular basis with their resourcefulness, humor, and energy.

My generous friends took the time to share their reflections, their advice, and their experience in reading this manuscript in its varying stages. Christopher Merrill, Mona Simpson, Mindy Goldberg, Kathy Braddock, Jenny Armit, Sean Elder, Helen Klein Ross, John Benditt, Peter Von Ziegesar, James Lister Smith, Sharon Rapoport, Elizabeth England, Merrill Feitell, Peter Moore, Angelica Baird, and Andrew Herwitz. My cousin Bruce Jones supplied family history. Writers are nourished by community, and so to my band of bros at 189, to Janis Andres and my tribe of superwomen in Los Angeles, and to my colleagues and students at the Todos Santos Writers Workshop, most especially my cherished collaborator and tireless supporter Rex Weiner, I am extremely grateful. Amy Gross, first editor and mentor, put in place many of the most important lessons I learned about voice and narrative. Elissa Schappell assigned the original essay that grew into this book, Sean Elder, Stephen P. Williams, and Cathleen Medwick also edited essays that knit their way in. Erin Rech and Jennifer Lambert Churchill taught me more about digital marketing than I thought I could possibly learn. Nina Subin generously took my photograph in her sublime studio. Finally, thanks are due to AWW, for his unerring ear, his great good humor, and for his ace coparenting.

Three writers, very dear friends no longer on this planet, live on forever in my heart: George Plimpton, Agha Shahid Ali, and James Salter. The elegance and economy of their work remain inspirational, as does every single word of advice they gave me, on both literary and life matters.

And to my family. It's never easy to have a writer in the clan, I get that. We each have our own version of events, and I'm grateful to you all, especially to my two sisters Darcy and Catherine, for giving me the space and the respect to tell mine.

About the Author

JEANNE MCCULLOCH is a former managing editor of the *Paris Review*, a former senior editor of *Tin House* magazine, and the founding editorial director of Tin House Books. She is a founding director of the Todos Santos Writers Workshop. Her writing has appeared in the *Paris Review*; *Tin House*; the *New York Times*; *O, The Oprah Magazine*; *Vogue*; *Allure*; and the *North American Review*, among other publications. She lives with her family in New York.